"Christianity is supernatural. We read the Bible and see God doing things that can't be explained rationally. That is the God we long for, One who can do extraordinary things in and around our ordinary lives. But Christianity is about God, not just what God does. I love this book, because Jared Wilson helps us worship the miracle worker, and not settle for just wanting and worshipping miracles."

   **Darrin Patrick,** Lead Pastor, The Journey, St. Louis, Missouri; Vice President, Acts 29; Chaplain to the St. Louis Cardinals; author, *The Dude's Guide to Manhood*

"Could it be that Jesus's miracles were not the paranormal, but actually the true normal breaking into our world of paranormal sin corruption? Wilson gets to the biblical heart of why Jesus performed miracles—these harbingers of God's mission to set right all that has gone so terribly wrong. Along the way, Wilson helps us hear what Jesus has to say to enlightened postmoderns, skeptics demanding apologetic proofs, and the paranormally fascinated. A soul-refreshing, gospel-drenched read."

   **Jon Bloom,** President, Desiring God; author, *Not by Sight* and *Things Not Seen*

"Jesus walked on water and healed the sick. He turned water into wine and raised men from the dead. How often we skim over these familiar stories, but as Jared Wilson writes, 'Miraculous events in the Bible are God putting an exclamation point where he normally puts a period.' *The Wonder-Working God* teaches us that these miracles aren't meant only to amaze us, they are to point us to Jesus Christ himself. I'm convinced I will never read about Jesus's life the same way again. Read it and think deeply about it as you glimpse the glory of Jesus—our Savior.

   **Trillia Newbell,** author, *United: Captured by God's Vision for Diversity*

"Jared Wilson brings his characteristic wit and careful exegesis to the often-misunderstood passages on God's miracles in a fresh and insightful way. *The Wonder-Working God* is a timely and necessary work for the church if we are going to better understand the workings of our great God in the present age."

   **Matt Carter,** Pastor of Preaching, The Austin Stone Community Church, Austin, Texas; author, *The Real Win*

"*Finally*, a treatment of Jesus's miracles that presents them more as a 'preview of coming attractions' and less as God's attempt to convince skeptics of his existence—as though God has ever 'attempted' to do anything. As Jared shows us, Jesus's miracles are more normal than we realize—an indicator of the way things used to be, before sin and death invaded God's story, and a precursor of the way things will be one day, when Jesus returns to finish making all things new."

   **Scotty Smith,** Teacher in Residence, West End Community Church, Nashville, Tennessee

"Into a world where naturalism is the prevailing philosophy, Jared Wilson casts a fresh vision for the wonder-working power of the God-man, Jesus of Nazareth. This biblically engaging, Christ-exalting, and never-boring book deserves your close and attentive reading."

**Sam Storms,** Senior Pastor, Bridgeway Church, Oklahoma City, Oklahoma

"Jared Wilson's crisp, potent, and winsome style portrays the Savior whose worth is magnified by his miraculous power. If you're holding this book, my advice is: Buy → Read → Wonder → Worship!"

**Dave Harvey,** Pastor of Preaching, Four Oaks Church; author, *When Sinners Say I Do* and *Am I Called?*

# THE WONDER-WORKING GOD

THE

# WONDER-WORKING
# GOD

Seeing the Glory of Jesus
in His Miracles

## Jared C. Wilson

CROSSWAY
WHEATON, ILLINOIS

*The Wonder-Working God: Seeing the Glory of Jesus in His Miracles*
Copyright © 2014 by Jared C. Wilson
Published by Crossway
    1300 Crescent Street
    Wheaton, Illinois 60187

Cover design: Faceout Studio, www.faceoutstudio.com

First printing 2014

Printed in the United States of America

Unless otherwise indicated, Scripture quotations are from the ESV® Bible (*The Holy Bible, English Standard Version®*), copyright © 2001 by Crossway. 2011 Text Edition. Used by permission. All rights reserved.

Scripture references marked NKJV are from *The New King James Version*. Copyright © 1982, Thomas Nelson, Inc. Used by permission.

Scripture quotations marked KJV are from the *King James Version* of the Bible.

All emphases in Scripture quotations have been added by the author.

Trade paperback ISBN: 978-1-4335-3672-4
ePub ISBN: 978-1-4335-3675-5
PDF ISBN: 978-1-4335-3673-1
Mobipocket ISBN: 978-1-4335-3674-8

**Library of Congress Cataloging-in-Publication Data**
Wilson, Jared C., 1975–
The wonder-working God : seeing the glory of Jesus in his miracles / Jared C. Wilson.
    pages cm
    Includes bibliographical references and index.
    ISBN 978-1-4335-3672-4 (tp)
    1. Jesus Christ—Miracles. 2. Bible—Criticism, interpre-
tation, etc. I. Title.
BT366.3.W55      2014
232.9'55—dc23               2013043732

Crossway is a publishing ministry of Good News Publishers.

| VP | | 23 | 22 | 21 | 20 | 19 | 18 | 17 | 16 | 15 | 14 |
|----|----|----|----|----|----|----|----|----|----|----|----|
| 15 | 14 | 13 | 12 | 11 | 10 | 9 | 8 | 7 | 6 | 5 | 4 | 3 | 2 | 1 |

For my precious chickadees, Macy and Grace.
May the miracle of greatest awe in your lives
continue forever to be the grace of God in
Christ given to you in Spiritual power

"When the real king emerges, however, and appears to view, things stand differently."

—Athanasius, *On the Incarnation*

# Contents

# Introduction

No one believes in miracles anymore. We are much too smart for that. The earth is round and our brains are evolved. Our creation is in the lab, our resurrection in the work of the microbiologist, our ascension in the journeys of the astronaut. Who needs revelation when we have the endless diversionary enlightenment of the Internet? Who needs prophets when we have experts?

Some scientists tell us that the things we often call miracles are statistical aberrations in the natural order of things, random outliers in the overwhelmingly "normal" flow of everyday events. Most say that what we label "a miracle" is simply an illusion, a trick on the eye, a misperception misattributed. Every event has a perfectly natural explanation, they say; we simply don't have all the data needed to explain what we've perceived. Scientism, which hinges on what may be observed, in this case insists that seeing is *not* believing. There are, then, rational explanations for every unexplained event, and the supernatural, by presupposition, cannot be one of them.

In this way, once again, science is pitted against religion, and to choose one is to disavow the other.

In the age of reality television and viral video, everything is extraordinary and therefore nothing is. We have no need for miracles, says the spirit of the age, because we are sufficiently advanced *and* entertained. Superstition is less and less acceptable as an explanation for the world and as an escape from the mundane life it offers.

Our miracles have become the stuff of sentiment, removed from the world of the supernatural and safely nestled in the inspirational world of human potential. In movies such as *Miracle on 34th Street* and *The Polar Express*, the power of belief becomes the miracle. "Anything's possible," goes the idea, "if you just believe." Many of us see this mantra repeated in a variety of ways every day in our Facebook newsfeeds and on Twitter.

The closest we may come to the miraculous in the popular imagination is the cultural fascination with the so-called paranormal. Vampires and zombies are the rage right now. Witches and warlocks appear to be in the next wave of occult appeal. When I was a kid, I consumed everything I could find related to UFOs, Bigfoot, and the Loch Ness Monster. Those sorts of speculative fiction are making comebacks still. My ten-year-old daughter loves the show *Fact or Faked*, wherein a team of special-effects experts and videographers examines videos of unexplained phenomena, then attempts to re-create the footage in a bid to conclude the veracity of the originals, or lack thereof. In nearly every case, they conclude that the video footage is the result of a perpetrated hoax or simple mistaken identity. However, the show succeeds not because it appeals to our inner skeptic but because it deftly raises our hopes for that one conclusive sign of something out there new, different, mysterious, out of the natural order—and real. On the popular television show *The X-Files*, FBI special agent Fox Mulder hung a now-iconic black-and-white poster on his office wall featuring a flying saucer and a caption reading, "I want to believe."

For all of our technological advances and instantaneous access to exhaustive information, we still carve out a space for the mysterious. Many of us say we don't. But we do. Some of our most ardent atheists have made clear their conditions for belief. They require a miracle. They don't believe in miracles, just as they don't believe in God, but if a miracle could be legitimately demonstrated, they claim, they would reverse their disbelief and agree that God exists.

But this is not how miracles ever worked. Even the miracles God grants to Moses in corroboration of his mission from *YHWH* to secure the children of Israel's release from bondage only serve to

harden Pharaoh's heart. Pharaoh says, "Prove yourselves" (Ex. 7:9),
but even when his demand is met, he is not satisfied (v. 13). When
God sends fire to consume Elijah's wet altar and shame the prophets
of Baal, there is no convincing anyone that *a* God exists but only
that "The LORD, he is God; the LORD, he is God" (1 Kings 18:39).

Further, in the New Testament accounts of Jesus's life and ministry, miracles seem to be plentiful, but none of them is meant to
convince his audiences that something like a god exists. Most of
them already believe that. And divine authenticity is only the tip
of the iceberg of the meaning of Jesus's miracles.

Certainly Jesus *is* God, and authenticating his deity is undoubtedly one of the functions of his miracles. But that is still scratching
the surface. Jesus himself rebukes the crowds that are looking for
signs. In one instance, he tells a parable of a dead man in the condemnation of hell begging Abraham for a resurrected witness to
evangelize his living relatives (Luke 16:19–31). Jesus has Abraham
tell the tortured man that unless there is belief in the Scriptures, a
miracle won't accomplish a thing (v. 31). Jesus later tells Thomas
that it is more blessed to believe *without* seeing (John 20:29).

The point is this: the miracles are more than they're cracked up
to be, but probably less than we often make of them. The miracles
are not the smoking gun, in other words. But they are the bright
explosions of the violent spiritual campaign against evil.

Even today, the New Testament miracles do not serve so much
to prove that there is a God but that the Lord is God and we are not.

It's a subtle distinction, to be sure, but the miracles in the Bible
never appear to serve God proving himself so much as God *showing*
himself. The Lord consistently refuses to be put on the defensive,
as if he must prove his existence to the jury of mortal disbelief in
order to save his life. Instead, he simply and majestically shows off.
And in the biblical economy of space-time—which is the actual
economy of space-time—what we eventually learn is that in a fallen
and broken world groaning for redemption, the miraculous *is* the
normal. By contrast, what we have come to call "normal life" is not

normal. Miracles don't turn things upside down, in other words, but rightside up.

I'll say more along those lines in chapter 1, but for the moment, let's consider this: What if the miracles in the Bible—and miracles today, should they still occur—are not God trying to convince us he's "up there somewhere," looming out there in heaven and trying on earth to get us to acknowledge him, but are actually God show-ing us that he is right here and right now in charge? What if, in other words, God is not an interloper in our world, but the things we find so familiarly "everyday"—sin, corruption, injustice, decay, death—these very "laws of nature," are interlopers in his?

When we are able to see the world that way, we get closer to the heart of the gospel. The miracles of Jesus serve that end, and when we see the world through the reality of the kingdom of God, the miracles become just as provocative, just as scandalous, in this day as they were in first-century Palestine. We post-postmoderns pride ourselves on being beyond all that superstitious hokum, but we place our hopes in the same sorts of sentimental magic as the ancients. We worship our accomplishments and our knowledge, be-cause we worship ourselves. It makes no difference that our golden calves are gadgets and Google, while their golden calves were, well, golden calves. There is nothing new under the sun, quantum me-chanics and particle physics notwithstanding. We seek a heaven on earth, be it natural or "supernatural," and we don't want this Jesus coming into the mix with his self-referential agitating. By reason and rationalization, we figure we can do just fine without him.

No, we don't believe in miracles anymore. We're much too smart for all that. But as it turns out, God's power is not hindered by disbelief. We don't believe in miracles. Well, okay. Turnabout is fair play, and the miracles don't believe in *us*.

The kingdom has come, is coming, and will come. You and I can-not impede this reality with our disbelief any more than we can en-hance it with our allegiance. Gravity did not become a law of nature when it was discovered. Who knows how many times that treasure in the field (Matt. 13:44) was trampled over before it was found?

The miracles do nothing for those who do not have the spiritual eyes to see them. Of the five thousand who ate Jesus's miracle meal in John 6, how many do you suppose remained after he began explaining the significance? It seems from the text only a few. Even some identified as disciples abandoned the mission (v. 66).

In some instances in the Gospels, the miracles have an effect also innate to the parables—confounding witnesses as much as enlightening them.

So we may keep building our Babel towers, be they monuments to religion or rationale, and even as we keep declaring our view of how the world is, we remain confused on the way it was meant to be. Our counterfeit heavens are both too earthy and not earthy enough. And part of God's plan in the revelation of the glory of his Son Jesus is to discredit and demolish both naturalistic utopia and Gnostic bliss. Somehow in the proclamation of the gospel of Christ and his kingdom is the merging of heaven and earth, in which each becomes what it was meant to be in relation to the other and each is revealed in the uniqueness of its truth and beauty.

The miracles speak to this reality. The real heaven. Heaven as it is, breaking in and bringing the light of truth. The real earth. Earth as it once was and as it will one day be—earth *as it is right now becoming*. The miracles of Jesus reveal what we go through such great pains to deny and what some of us go through great pains to affirm. The miracles present the vision of what every human heart is yearning for.

Heaven on earth. Can it be?

# 1

# Windows into Heaven

In Rob Reiner's film adaptation of William Goldman's book *The Princess Bride*, comedian Billy Crystal plays Miracle Max, a crusty peasant known for his homegrown remedies. The hero, Westley, his friends believe, is dead, and they take him to Miracle Max in the hope of having him revived. The scene that ensues is one of the highlights of the story and gives rise to one of the more quotable lines in a movie full of quotable lines: "It just so happens that your friend here is only *mostly* dead. There's a big difference between mostly dead and all dead."

After a hilarious process of diagnosis involving a fireplace bellows and the harangues of Max's hideous wife, the protagonists receive an antidote and Westley eventually lives to fight another day. This homeopathic remedy, some dubious alchemist's concoction, is what passes for a miracle in the medieval fantasy world of Florin.

As a pastor, I hear numerous requests for prayer every week. As I write this chapter, in fact, I am in the cafeteria of our local hospital, waiting for one of our church members to finish his nap so I can visit with him. He fell off a ladder last night and broke some bones in his leg. We will be praying for his healing. This healing will likely occur through the combined processes of medical treatment and time. Even this normal healing we will consider the work of God. But we won't use the word *miracle* to describe his healing unless something out of the ordinary takes place to accomplish it.

The surgery he is scheduled to undergo tomorrow probably won't qualify. When I go upstairs to check on him in an hour or so and we pray for his comfort and restoration, if his bones were to be repaired instantaneously, we would definitely call that a miracle. Anything short of that, however, would feel too much like cheapening the word.

Many others in our culture feel no such compunction. "Choose your miracle." "Every day is a miracle." Phrases like these and others proliferate in both spiritual and secular Western culture, popularized on TBN or the *Oprah* show. In this milieu, a miracle is a fulfillment of your personal dreams and ambitions, and the accumulation of accolades and treasures.

None of this is miraculous in the biblical sense because it remains disconnected from the glory of Jesus Christ. The biblical miracles happened to reveal something about Jesus. When the charlatan on television tells you to sow a financial seed in expectation of a monetary windfall, it is not a miracle he is suggesting, but magic—witchcraft, to be more specific. The products of these so-called miracles are things Jesus consistently warned us about, temporary treasures that degrade our souls when trusted.

In the Bible, a miracle involves transformation from death to life or from nothing to something. But in the modern world, *miracle* simply means "easy," "convenient," or "quick." The word *miracle* gets trotted out about everything from pharmaceuticals to exercise plans. The miracle drugs of contemporary culture are magic beans. And more often than not, they serve only to exalt their recipient. Today's signs only signify themselves.

Not so the signs of Jesus. His miracles were not ends in and of themselves. They were flaming arrows pointing back to him and the quality of his kingship. The recipients of Jesus's miracles were often warned not to terminate on the wonders, in fact, but on the worker. While today's puny miracles tell the story of human comfort and self-actualization, the biblical miracles tell another story, one about the central figure in the story of the entire cosmos. It is only this story, in fact, that solves the essential human problem.

See, we are not "mostly dead" creatures needing some refreshment. The way even many Christian ministries teach the Bible lends credence to the idea that we're really just a little confused, a bit hobbled, simply unsophisticated, untrained, and uninformed. If we just had the right tools and techniques, we could be successful and victorious. Not only are we not "mostly dead," we learn, but "mostly alive." We just need some spiritual spritzer, some kind of "Jesusy" pick-me-up.

The true gospel assumes, however, that we are not "mostly alive" or even "mostly dead," but all the way dead. Worse than dead, even, if the depiction of our state in Ephesians 2:1–3 is accurate. Apart from Christ, we are animalistic, Devil-following, world-captured, wrath-deserving spiritual corpses. The unparalleled severity of our dilemma requires an eternally powerful antidote. It is this situation on a global scale that the gospel of the kingdom addresses.

## The Gospel of the Kingdom

The biblical Gospels tell us that Jesus came preaching "the gospel of the kingdom of God" (with Matthew often employing "heaven" as a respectful circumlocution for "God"). This is the message Jesus charged his disciples to proclaim as well. In the Gospels of Matthew and Mark, in fact, we learn that the kingdom is "at hand."

What does all of this mean?

The kingdom of God, first of all, is this: the manifest presence of God's sovereignty. That is, it is the reign of God being brought to bear among people and cultures in creation. God has never *not* reigned, of course. He has always been God, declaring the end from the beginning, hardening whom he wills and having mercy on whom he wills, overseeing both good and bad. There is no thwarting of his sovereign will. But in the proclamation of his kingdom, something special, something different, is happening.

The reign of God is finally and directly being pressed into the brokenness of the world—the sins of men and the rebellion and injustice of mankind—fulfilling God's promise to one day set things back to rights.

The church often gets "the kingdom" wrong, because we equate it so often with the church or with the place of paradise we call heaven. But while both the church and heaven are integral to the purposes of God's kingdom, neither is itself the kingdom. The kingdom is God's reign, his sovereignty, his will being done. And in the case of the covenantal climax of the Gospels, the kingdom coming is God's will finally being done on earth as it is in heaven.

The kingdom coming is no scheme of man, however. We cannot orchestrate it or manage it. The kingdom must come from God himself. Enter the God-man, Jesus the Christ. He is the long-awaited Messiah, the Son of Man and the Son of God, the King of kings. The kingdom of God broke into the world in and through the person of Jesus. There can be no kingdom without a king, and ours comes announcing that God is now forgiving sins, restoring peace and justice, reversing the curse, and setting in motion the end of days. This is—finally—good news for a creation that is groaning for redemption. All that is left for us to do is repent and believe, and the kingdom blessings will be ours, too. But only through Jesus. No Jesus, no blessing.

You would think this good news would have struck everyone who heard it as good news indeed, but, of course, most of us know that it did not. Many people hated Jesus, and even those indifferent to him conspired in his execution. So why didn't they recognize his greatness and the greatness of his news?

The aversion to Jesus in the Gospels played on a few levels. Some were afraid of following him into hardship and death. Some did not see how his way of reigning—through serving and suffering—could possibly compute with their expectations of what the Messiah would do. Some did not like the way he questioned the existing religious authorities, as he frequently challenged, rebuked, and embarrassed them. Some did not like the company he kept and preferred the comfort of their own pride and arrogance. Some just could not see him for who he truly was.

But all of these positions had one thing in common, and it is this one thing that resulted in condemnation. Each was a fundamental rejection of Jesus as Lord. Nothing short of trust in Jesus Christ results in salvation. This is why the good news of the kingdom compels those who *see Jesus as he is* to repent of their old, normal ways of doing humanity and follow his new, supernatural way.

## The Kingdom Story

The Bible opens with the formation of the world, and from the start God exercises his sovereign power and authority in separating light from darkness (Gen. 1:4), the skies from the seas (vv. 7–8), and the land from the waters (v. 9). The divine edicts are perfectly obeyed as our God creates the world *ex nihilo*. In the continuation of creation, God establishes a creation *order*, placing mankind above the animals (v. 26), declaring the husband as head of the wife (2:18–22; Eph. 5:23), and giving the first couple dominion under his authority over the earth, with a charge to be fruitful and multiply, and to tend the garden and subdue the earth (Gen. 1:28–29; 2:15). In other words, as a reflection of God's own inter-Trinitarian activity and outward creative nature, Adam and Eve are commanded to collaborate, create, and cultivate.

The whole creation and the order established to cultivate it into the future is declared "good" by God. The elements and the systems needed for perfect peace are all present. Why? Because it is all as God means for it to be, perfectly aligned under his sovereign will and design. The kingdom of God is manifested in great harmony with the created world.

But as in every powerful story, a crisis arises. The king's subjects, led astray by the satanic tempter, rebel against the divine authority, committing treason in their disobedience (3:1–13). The perfect alignment between kingdom and creation is shifted. *Shalom* is shattered.

The result is all creation under a curse (vv. 14–19) and mankind forced into a sort of exile from being "at home" in the world (vv. 23–24). All the aching for more, the longing for purpose, the search for meaning, the desire for justice and peace comes from this original fracture. Adam and Eve disobey God, and the rest is sordid history.

But there is something curious in the story of the fall, in the very explication of the curse. Embedded in the consequences of sin is the shadow of a hope for a remedy:

The LORD God said to the serpent,

"Because you have done this,
  cursed are you above all livestock
  and above all beasts of the field;
on your belly you shall go,
  and dust you shall eat
  all the days of your life.
I will put enmity between you and the woman,
  and between your offspring and her offspring;
he shall bruise your head,
  and you shall bruise his heel." (vv. 14–15)

The tempter is cursed, too. And in his curse lies what some theologians call the proto-evangelium, or "first gospel." Man will bruise the Serpent's head, and the Serpent will bruise man's heel. This may be a forecast of the crucifixion of the Messiah, Jesus. His death will appear to be the fatal strike of the Serpent, but in fact will be the decisive crushing of the Serpent's head.

What an interesting irony! What is meant as defeat by the rebellious glory-thieves turns out to be victory for the King! This inside-out, rightside-up twist in the story is described in a variety of ways in the Bible. The crucifixion of the King becomes his conquest. The prophet Isaiah promises that "upon him was the chastisement that brought us peace, and with his wounds we are healed" (53:5). The apostle Paul writes about this juxtaposition this way:

And you, who were dead in your trespasses and the uncircumcision of your flesh, God made alive together with him,

having forgiven us all our trespasses, by canceling the record
of debt that stood against us with its legal demands. This he
set aside, nailing it to the cross. He disarmed the rulers and
authorities and put them to open shame, by triumphing over
them in him. (Col. 2:13–15)

The cross, seen by worldly eyes as the symbol of crushing defeat, becomes the means of Satan-vanquishing, law-fulfilling, sin-
conquering, life-giving power.

But as in any great, masterful story, there is yet another twist,
something hardly anyone can see coming. God's kingdom has more
to conquer. So while the cross becomes the means of triumph over
sin, it is retroactively made so because of what comes next, the
great eucatastrophe of human history: the resurrection of Jesus
Christ:

> But in fact Christ has been raised from the dead, the firstfruits
> of those who have fallen asleep. For as by a man came death,
> by a man has come also the resurrection of the dead. For as
> in Adam all die, so also in Christ shall all be made alive. But
> each in his own order: Christ the firstfruits, then at his com-
> ing those who belong to Christ. Then comes the end, when he
> delivers the kingdom to God the Father after destroying every
> rule and every authority and power. For he must reign until
> he has put all his enemies under his feet. The last enemy to be
> destroyed is death. For "God has put all things in subjection
> under his feet." But when it says, "all things are put in sub-
> jection," it is plain that he is excepted who put all things in
> subjection under him. When all things are subjected to him,
> then the Son himself will also be subjected to him who put
> all things in subjection under him, that God may be all in all.
> (1 Cor. 15:20–28)

Adam's sin brings death into the world. And only death can
take it out (Heb. 9:22). But God is not content with this eye-for-
an-eye stuff. His plan is not amelioration but restoration, renewal.

Death must itself be banished to set God's creation order back fully to rights.

From reign to chaos to rescue. This is God's plan for the world, and it is the story the Bible tells from cover to cover, beginning with the tragic fall in Genesis and culminating in the final, consummate victory of Jesus Christ over injustice, wickedness, and death in Revelation.

We live now, as every Christian has until now, in the "end times," the momentary waiting between Christ's inauguration of the kingdom through his incarnation, death, resurrection, and ascension, and Christ's consummation of the kingdom through his future return. The kingdom has come and is coming still. It comes, in fact, very powerfully, violently even, and those desperate for its presence lay hold of it with passionate force (Matt. 11:12). It is this creation-shaking power that we see in all kingdom activity.

Because the entire world has been affected by mankind's sin, the way the Bible talks about the kingdom's coming seems somewhat cataclysmic. This place is broken, but because we have become so accustomed to living with the brokenness, the very restoration of the place can seem like a breaking. And it is. It is a breaking of the way things have been and a resetting to the way they ought to be. The prophet Daniel interprets a rather disturbing dream for King Nebuchadnezzar this way:

> You, O king, the king of kings, to whom the God of heaven has given the kingdom, the power, and the might, and the glory, and into whose hand he has given, wherever they dwell, the children of man, the beasts of the field, and the birds of the heavens, making you rule over them all—you are the head of gold. Another kingdom inferior to you shall arise after you, and yet a third kingdom of bronze, which shall rule over all the earth. And there shall be a fourth kingdom, strong as iron, because iron breaks to pieces and shatters all things. And like iron that crushes, it shall break and crush all these. And as you saw the feet and toes, partly of potter's clay and partly of

iron, it shall be a divided kingdom, but some of the firmness of iron shall be in it, just as you saw iron mixed with the soft clay. And as the toes of the feet were partly iron and partly clay, so the kingdom shall be partly strong and partly brittle. As you saw the iron mixed with soft clay, so they will mix with one another in marriage, but they will not hold together, just as iron does not mix with clay. And in the days of those kings the God of heaven will set up a kingdom that shall never be destroyed, nor shall the kingdom be left to another people. It shall break in pieces all these kingdoms and bring them to an end, and it shall stand forever. (Dan. 2:37–44)

As mighty and as expansive as Nebuchadnezzar's kingdom was, and other great earthly kingdoms have been and will be, they are as nothing compared to the kingdom of God, the eternal kingdom that will never be destroyed because it is built by God himself. Its entrance into the world is depicted as breaking all the other kingdoms into pieces and reducing them to nothing.

Similarly, the prophet Isaiah forecasts the coming of the kingdom through the Messiah's reign this way:

A voice cries:
"In the wilderness prepare the way of the Lord;
   make straight in the desert a highway for our God.
Every valley shall be lifted up,
   and every mountain and hill be made low;
the uneven ground shall become level,
   and the rough places a plain.
And the glory of the Lord shall be revealed,
   and all flesh shall see it together,
   for the mouth of the Lord has spoken." (Isa. 40:3–5)

The coming of the King is seen as an "earth-shattering" event. The reversal depicted here is emblematic of the kingdom's reversing of the curse. This is the passage that John the Baptist employs to herald the coming of his cousin Jesus (Luke 3:2–6).

The manifest presence of God's sovereignty has huge ramifications—not just for the fallen creation, but for the corrupt systems, the injustice and broken *shalom* among nations and peoples. Consider yet another kingdom prophecy from Isaiah:

> The Spirit of the Lord GOD is upon me,
>   because the LORD has anointed me
> to bring good news to the poor;
>   he has sent me to bind up the brokenhearted,
> to proclaim liberty to the captives,
>   and the opening of the prison to those who are bound;
> to proclaim the year of the LORD's favor,
>   and the day of vengeance of our God;
>   to comfort all who mourn;
> to grant to those who mourn in Zion—
>   to give them a beautiful headdress instead of ashes,
> the oil of gladness instead of mourning,
>   the garment of praise instead of a faint spirit;
> that they may be called oaks of righteousness,
>   the planting of the LORD, that he may be glorified.
> They shall build up the ancient ruins;
>   they shall raise up the former devastations;
> they shall repair the ruined cities,
>   the devastations of many generations. (Isa. 61:1–4)

This is the very text that Jesus reads in the synagogue and then ascribes to himself (Luke 4:16–21).

These passages are just a sampling of the way the Bible tells the fantastic story of the kingdom. In review: God makes everything, and he makes it good. The sin of mankind corrupts everything, breaking our world and our very selves. But God does not let our sin have the last word. He intervenes himself, sending his Son to proclaim the climactic arrival of his kingdom and himself as King, which is ultimately ratified and actualized through his death and resurrection, and which promises not just a return to the way things used to be but a renewal, a restoration of creation as even "better than good." It is not Eden's garden we long for now but the new heaven and the new earth. Therefore, the mission of the church today is to continue proclaiming Christ as King and the "at hand"-ness of his kingdom, which promises to anyone who repents and believes in Jesus pardon from sins and victory over death through everlasting union with him.

That, in a nutshell, is the story of the kingdom. It is the story the books of the Old Testament forecast and anticipate. It is the story the New Testament assumes and proclaims. It is the story the four Gospels begin, each in its own idiosyncratic way.

In a previous book, I addressed the role of Jesus's parables in this story, asking in effect, "What purpose do Jesus's little stories serve in the bigger story of the kingdom?" My argument throughout that work was that the parables reveal (or conceal, depending on the prerogative of the Spirit) the glory of Jesus Christ in service to the mission of his kingdom.

The question in this book is this: "How do Jesus's *miracles* fit in the kingdom story?" But before we answer that question, we have to answer a more primary one.

## What Are Miracles?

We tend to think of miracles as "special" things God does on occasion, things really out of the ordinary. This is a perfectly understandable definition, but the problem of thinking about miracles entirely this way ought to be apparent—it lends itself to the idea that some things God does aren't special, that some things he does are ordinary. But nothing God does can be thought to be mundane. Everything he does is exciting, from the raising of the dead to the raising of the farmer's crops.

God cannot be boring. If we find him boring, it is we who are the problem, not God. He does not sometimes do marvelous things and sometimes dull things. No, the real difference is in our failure to marvel. The heavens we walk under every day declare the glory of God. This is a miracle.

But of course, expanding our view of the miraculous to *everything* runs that previously discouraged risk of cheapening the very word *miracle*. If we can agree that nothing God does is essentially boring—that, in fact, his very existence and presence in the world mean life cannot be boring—can we still set aside certain events from the ordinary run of affairs as miraculous? I think so.

Here is a survey of how a few modern sources have defined the word *miracle*:

- [T]he biblical concept of a miracle is that of an event which runs counter to the observed processes of nature.—*Evangelical Dictionary of Theology*[1]
- In biblical scholarship the English word *miracle* normally denotes a supernatural event, that is, an event which so transcends ordinary happenings that it is viewed as a direct result of supernatural power.—*Dictionary of Jesus and the Gospels*[2]
- [E]ven the loosest use of the term "miracle" normally designates something distinct from God's ordinary activity in the universe.—Craig S. Keener[3]
- The divine art of miracle is not an art of suspending the pattern to which events conform but of feeding new events into that pattern.—C. S. Lewis[4]

Each of these definitions provides a valuable facet to a whole understanding, each being right in its own respect. For the purpose of this work, I propose this general working definition of *miracle*: a supernatural act of God that glorifies Jesus.

But this definition requires a definition of its own. By *supernatural*, I refer to the acts of God in and through nature that appear to suspend or override the ordinarily observable patterns of nature. Lewis explains:

---

[1] J. D. Spiceland, "Miracle," in *Evangelical Dictionary of Theology*, 2nd ed., ed. Walter A. Elwell (Grand Rapids, MI: Baker, 2001), 779.
[2] B. L. Blackburn, "Miracles and Miracle Stories," in *Dictionary of Jesus and the Gospels*, ed. Joel B. Green, Scot McKnight, and I. Howard Marshall (Downers Grove, IL: InterVarsity, 1992), 549.
[3] Craig S. Keener, *Miracles: The Credibility of the New Testament Accounts*, vol. 1 (Grand Rapids, MI: Baker, 2011), 182.
[4] C. S. Lewis, *Miracles: A Preliminary Study* (New York: HarperCollins, 2001), 95.

The experience of a miracle in fact requires two conditions. First we must believe in a normal stability of nature, which means we must recognize that the data offered by our senses recur in regular patterns. Second, we must believe in some reality beyond Nature.[5]

At the same time, however, we must stress that to say a miracle derives from beyond nature does not mean it is an infraction against nature, as if nature is the rule and God the exception. Some thinkers define *miracles* as violations of the "laws of nature," but we ought to reject this definition because it posits God as some kind of cosmic vandal or rogue prankster. Continuing with Lewis:

> It is therefore inaccurate to define a miracle as something that breaks the laws of Nature. It doesn't. If I knock out my pipe I alter the position of a great many atoms. . . . Nature digests or assimilates this event with perfect ease and harmonises it in a twinkling with all other events. It is one more bit of raw material for the laws to apply to, and they apply. . . . If events ever come from beyond Nature altogether, she will be no more incommoded by them. Be sure she will rush to the point where she is invaded, as the defensive forces rush to a cut in our finger, and there hasten to accommodate the newcomer. The moment it enters her realm it obeys all her laws.[6]

Lewis goes on to say that miraculous wine can make one drunk and miraculous bread can be eaten. So when we think of miracles as supernatural, we must not think of them as essentially counternatural. They are otherworldly—even counter-worldly by the biblical definition of *worldly*—but they are very much expressions within nature, having natural effects, not violating nature but adjusting its pattern, making nature in fact larger, more vivid, more *real*—more submissive to its Creator.

[5] C. S. Lewis, "Miracles," in *God in the Dock: Essays on Theology and Ethics* (Grand Rapids, MI: Eerdmans, 1993), 27.
[6] Lewis, *Miracles*, 94–95.

No, while miracles cannot rightly be thought of as ordinary, they still cannot be thought of as violations of natural law. If they violate anything, it is our perceptions, assumptions, and sensibilities, all of which are immanently fallible. Fifteen hundred years before Lewis, St. Augustine employed this biblical logic in his *City of God*:

> For we say that all portents are contrary to nature; but they are not so. For how is that contrary to nature which happens by the will of God, since the will of so mighty a Creator is certainly the nature of each created thing? A portent, therefore, happens not contrary to nature, but contrary to what we know as nature.[7]

In the Scriptures, God performs certain acts, it seems, only on special occasions. Some occasionally ask why we see so many miracles in the Bible and so few in "real life" today, but we ought to remember that the Bible does not record every day of its history, and even many of its recorded days passed by sans miracles. In the Scriptures, we have a representative highlighting of the mighty acts of God in his relationship with his covenant people. The miracles, as it were, are bunched up in the Bible because they were deemed more worthy of recording for posterity than the things that happened on the more ordinary days. Again, we have plenty of those recorded in the Bible, too, so we should not assume from the proliferation of the miracles in the Scriptures the commonness of them.

As the story of the Scriptures progresses, however, miracles seem to become more frequent, culminating in Jesus's earthly ministry. Lewis puts the miracles in the context of the kingdom story: "The miracles in fact are a retelling in small letters of the very same story which is written across the whole world in letters too large for some of us to see."[8]

Then we see this: not miracles as strange interruptions of the

---

[7] Augustine, *City of God*, 21.8, trans. Marcus Dods (New York: Random House, 1950), 776.
[8] Lewis, "Miracles," 29.

normal world but miracles as normal interruptions of a strange world. We begin our consideration of Jesus's ministry with the biblical belief that the world is broken because of sin, that it is fractured and indeed groaning, that what we see, as beautiful as it is, is still not right. The earth is aching for God's righteousness. Then comes Jesus Christ, bending, it seems, the very laws of nature. In fact, he is straightening them out.

In this sense, it is the world as it is that is not normal, and the miracles exist as great demonstrations of normalization! Heaven is the place where God's will is done perfectly, and the prayer of our Lord is that the earth will be aligned with heaven in that way, that God's will should be done here just as it is there.

What are the miracles, then, but glimpses of the way the world is meant to be, glimpses of the way the world is actually becoming? In and through Jesus, the kingdom is coming, and God's will is being done on earth as it is done in heaven. Jesus's miracles are the very windows into heaven, and through them heaven is spilling into earth like sunlight through panes whose shades have been violently rolled up.

## What Do Christ's Miracles Do?

The miraculous events in the Bible are God putting an exclamation point where he normally puts a period. Through the light of the New Testament, we know that even the Old Testament miracles are supernatural acts of God meant to glorify Jesus. But when we get to the ministry of Jesus in the Gospels, it seems as if a dam has broken and the water of the miraculous is rushing. Crowds of people flock to Jesus because they expect from him what by definition should be unexpected.

But Jesus rarely rewards the sinner's search for parlor tricks. In this knowledge, it is important to distinguish the supernatural work of God meant to glorify Jesus and the supernatural work of satanic spirits meant to counterfeit the kingdom and deceive observers. These dark demonstrations may generally qualify as miraculous, but they are more rightly thought of as magic, which is something the Bible forbids and warns against.

What Jesus performs, however, are the genuine articles— supernatural acts of God through himself as King (and subsequently through his subjects) meant to glorify his kingship and reveal certain truths about his kingdom. And setting aside a few occasions when the absence of faith precludes them, Jesus seems to perform miracles whenever he wishes.

Today some argue that Jesus performed miracles precisely to attract crowds, so that people could then hear his important teachings. But Jesus seemed decidedly against using his power as some sort of gospel bait and switch. His ministry was not the proto- "seeker church."

Some also say Jesus's miracles were meant to authenticate his deity. As we have discussed, there are shades of truth to this idea, but it is not the whole reality. The miracles were not meant to be lures or attractants. They were instances of the kingdom's invasion of fallen creation, those "windows into heaven" mentioned above, portals through which the thicker, realer space of heaven was rushing into the thinner space of earth. Thomas Schreiner puts it this way: "Jesus' miracles . . . are themselves the actualization, at least in part, of the kingdom."[9] Or, as Craig Blomberg suggests, "Miracles were, in a sense, enacted metaphors of God's sovereignty."[10] In other words, the miracles are pictures of what happens when God's will is manifest on earth as it is in heaven.

We hear the tones of this miraculous presence in what might be called Jesus's "lesser" miracles: his acts of prescience, prophecy, and preaching with authority. But we see vivid examples of the manifest presence of God's sovereignty in four major categories of Jesus's miracles, and then what we might call the special case. This book will largely follow this categorical trajectory: Christ's control over nature (chaps. 2–4), Christ's healings (chaps. 5–6), Christ's ex-

---

[9] Thomas R. Schreiner, *New Testament Theology: Magnifying God in Christ* (Grand Rapids, MI: Baker, 2008), 64.
[10] Craig L. Blomberg, *Jesus and the Gospels: An Introduction and Survey* (Nashville: Broadman and Holman, 1997), 67.

orcisms (chap. 7), Christ's resurrections (chaps. 8–9), and the special case of his very self (chap. 10).

All of the miracles in these categories are not simple authentications of Jesus's deity but demonstrations of the divine in the world at that time, proclamations in deed of the divine purpose for the world. And so we see the miracles not as some acts Jesus conjured up, not as a garland of tricks simply adorning his ministry, but as the inevitable trail of effects of the kingdom breaking into the world.

Benjamin B. Warfield writes: "When our Lord came down to earth He drew heaven with Him. The signs which accompanied His ministry were but the trailing clouds of glory which He brought from heaven, which is His home."[11]

Because Jesus's very person was the perfect integration of full humanity and full divinity, he carried around with him the growing rift between this world and that one. As he walked, his elbows traced both the air and the ether, stretching the limits of creation, the heavenly gravity pressing in at his movements. Jesus strained the capacity of this world with his very presence. The world's breeches were too small, in other words, for the King of the universe, and we should not be surprised that as the seams split, glory streamed through.

What do Jesus's miracles do? Primarily four things:

- The miracles demonstrate the "at hand"-ness of the kingdom of God.
- The miracles are acts of heavenly *normalization*, which is to say they are isolated snapshots of the transformation of the broken world to the way it will someday be.
- Because the miracles are acts of heavenly normalization, they are acts of revolutionary subversion against the corrupt course of the world and the realm of the Evil One.
- The miracles point to Jesus Christ himself as the source and summation of the three acts above.

---

[11] Benjamin B. Warfield, *Counterfeit Miracles* (New York: Scribner's, 1918), 3.

These four primary effects of the miracles in the Gospels are the ways they reveal the glory of the Son of God, and we will see how the various miracles evince these purposes with varying emphases.

Jesus's miracles make good on the covenantal promises of abundance, peace, and even immortality bound up in allegiance to God. The miracles show us Eden but greater. They show us the sinless Adam but better. The miracles reveal the glory, the beholding of which makes dying sinners become like the unconquerable Christ.

# 2

# A Bottle of the Good Stuff

I performed my first miracle at the age of nineteen. To this date, it is my only miracle, but I carried it out to great effect and much acclaim.

I was an intern for a student ministry in Houston, Texas, and was leading the Wednesday night youth service for the umpteenth time. Leading this service always involved ever-increasing anxiety about coming up with something fresh and engaging for the hundred or so kids from seventh through twelfth grades. I had run out of clever alliterations that night, I assume, so I decided to work a miracle.

I turned water into wine.

The kids were restless, as usual, hopped up on Pixy Stix and Coca-Cola and eight verses of "Zoom around the Room and Praise the Lord." With knees goose-pimpled and knocking from the frigid air-conditioning in our "JAM Room"—Jesus and Me, don't you know?—they watched curiously from their uncomfortable metal chairs as I approached a table set on the stage before them.

On the table sat two pitchers and one glass. One of the pitchers was empty. The other was full of water. I began to teach on Jesus's miracle at the wedding at Cana, and before all their wide eyes and gaping mouths, I poured the water from one pitcher to another, where it visibly turned to "red wine."

Only one kid asked how I did it. I told him, "The Lord."

Really, what no one could see, even from the front row closest to the table, was the thin pool of purple food coloring at the bottom of the empty pitcher. As the poured liquid merged with the dye, it instantly turned a bright shade of purple.

But I knew I had to give more oomph to the trick. I poured some of the miracle beverage into a glass and handed it to a middle-school boy on the front row, assuring the good Baptist youth leaders in the room that it was non-alcoholic. The kid looked frightened, as if I was trying to poison him. "Go ahead," I said.

He sipped.

"Well," I asked, "what does it taste like?"

"Grape juice."

The crowd gasped. (Or, at least, I imagined they did.)

Voila. I had turned water into wine.

It helps to pull this off if you not only use unnoticeable food coloring at the bottom of your empty pitcher, but also make sure your "water" is white grape juice. In an off-color translucent pitcher, white grape juice looks plenty like water.

I don't remember the bulk of my message that night, but I remember performing this illusion and I remember the point of making the kid drink the wine. I said something like, "It's not enough to simply look transformed; you have to be transformed." I tied that point into a warning against the tendency for church kids to "play Christian," to go through the motions or something like that. I am fairly positive it was the best inspirational legalism I could gin up at the time, but I think that the fundamental point still holds true, and I think it holds true in the actual miracle of our Lord at Cana, my past butchering of the application notwithstanding. One may give the appearance of truth while remaining essentially false.

This is a point Jesus repeated throughout his teaching ministry, from his condemning of whitewashed tombs and criticizing of outwardly clean dishes (Matt. 23:25–27) to his cursing of the leafy-but-fruitless fig tree (Mark 11:12–14) and calling out of heartless lip-syncing (Mark 7:6).

When the Son of God dropped into history, the Jewish people had already long been infected by false fronts and spiritual playacting. The harsh words of Isaiah 58 and the entire book of Malachi are just two notable indications. The religious establishment especially had become expert at managing appearances, projecting a respectable facade of faithfulness.

A friend's wife was a student witness to the 1970 revival at Asbury College. Unanticipated and unorchestrated, the Spirit seemed to baptize the worshipers at the school with powerful love, a deeper sense of his presence in the gospel. The believers were broken open in repentance and reconciliation, and were further empowered in confidence and evangelism. Spontaneous weeping and singing marked the gatherings. Even those most prone toward skepticism of such things on campus were convinced this was a genuine and fresh move of God. The movement lasted approximately 144 uninterrupted hours, during which business as usual at the school essentially stopped.

Then, my friend's wife said, something changed. Almost as soon as it came, the revival seemed to go. And yet some were tempted to keep it going under their own power. They wanted to prolong the special presence with manufactured emotions and responses. College leaders wisely squelched the opportunity for the counterfeit, instructing all the students to return to their classes and resume their normal schedules.

The religious climate of Jesus's day was evidence of what happens when no one stops the counterfeit. The Spirit of God had gone silent after Malachi, but that did not stop the spiritual authorities from trying to keep the whole mechanism turning under the power of their own self-righteousness. Can you imagine what it might be like to have been faking spiritual power for hundreds of years when suddenly the real thing shows up? John the Baptist assumes the prophetic mantle, preparing the way for the Lord himself to come crashing through the facades, breaking the bonds of the spiritual captives with triumph. What would that be like?

Maybe it would be a little like bringing a glass of what you expect to be tepid water to your mouth and being startled when wine hits your lips—the strong kind.

## The Life of the Party

Since the Bible's great story of redemption begins with a wedding (Gen. 2:22–24) and ends with a wedding (Rev. 19:6–9), it makes sense that Christ commences his public ministry at a wedding. Marriage becomes a dominant image representing God's love for his people, and thus the image of the groom finally joining his bride becomes emblematic of Christ's coming for his church and even the kingdom's joyous (re)union with creation.

It is perhaps this latter image that John has most in mind in his Gospel, as he begins with a glorious echo of creation:

> In the beginning was the Word, and the Word was with God, and the Word was God. He was in the beginning with God. All things were made through him, and without him was not any thing made that was made. In him was life, and the life was the light of men. The light shines in the darkness, and the darkness has not overcome it. (John 1:1–5)

John 1:10 tells us that the world was created through the Son of God, which shows that he was present and active long before his incarnation and therefore eternally coexistent with the Father, *that he is God* just as the Father and the Spirit are God. John makes explicit what is more implicit in the Synoptic Gospels—the Word of the Old Testament's creation story is the Jesus of the New Testament's *new* creation story. The Gospels, in fact, are chronicling the coming of the kingdom of God in and through Jesus Christ as the dawning of the renewal of all things (Rev. 21:5). And just as Genesis 1:9–13 records the setting aside of the waters and the bringing forth of fruit on the third day, John records the following:

> On the third day there was a wedding at Cana in Galilee, and the mother of Jesus was there. Jesus also was invited to

the wedding with his disciples. When the wine ran out, the mother of Jesus said to him, "They have no wine." And Jesus said to her, "Woman, what does this have to do with me? My hour has not yet come." His mother said to the servants, "Do whatever he tells you."

Now there were six stone water jars there for the Jewish rites of purification, each holding twenty or thirty gallons. Jesus said to the servants, "Fill the jars with water." And they filled them up to the brim. And he said to them, "Now draw some out and take it to the master of the feast." So they took it. When the master of the feast tasted the water now become wine, and did not know where it came from (though the servants who had drawn the water knew), the master of the feast called the bridegroom and said to him, "Everyone serves the good wine first, and when people have drunk freely, then the poor wine. But you have kept the good wine until now." This, the first of his signs, Jesus did at Cana in Galilee, and manifested his glory. And his disciples believed in him. (John 2:1–11)

Last things first. John tells us the purpose of this miracle, which happens to be the purpose of all Jesus's miracles. Jesus's purpose is this: to manifest his glory. Rudolf Schnackenburg concurs, writing, "The most important [thought] for the evangelist is the revelation of Jesus's glory . . . and any interpretation which departs from this Christological perspective loses sight of the central issue."[1] We identify this purpose first, in other words, to help prevent us from fanciful understandings of the miracle that would take us far afield from the substance of the gospel. It would be a dangerous mistake, in fact, to behold the miracle while failing to behold Christ. D. A. Carson reminds us, "The servants saw the sign, but not the glory; the disciples by faith perceived Jesus's glory behind the sign, and they *put their faith in him*."[2]

[1] Rudolf Schnackenburg, *The Gospel According to St. John*, vol. I (London: Burns & Oates, 1968), 337, quoted in Craig L. Blomberg, "The Miracles as Parables," *Gospel Perspectives*, vol. 6: *The Miracles of Jesus* (Sheffield, England: JSOT Press, 1986), 334.
[2] D. A. Carson, *The Gospel according to John* (Grand Rapids, MI: Eerdmans, 1998), 175. Emphasis original.

But what does this miracle reveal about Jesus? What of his glory is to be seen in it?

We certainly see Jesus's power. He can make something exist that did not exist. The jars are filled with water and Jesus makes them filled with wine. Whether he does it with a word or a movement, we don't know. The text doesn't say. All we are left with is the understanding that the servants pour in water and ladle out wine. Jesus's creative power is astounding.

At this point, many teachers highlight that Jesus was at a party, so he must have been a, you know, party animal or something. He liked to hang out at parties and drink, they remind us.

This may be one of the dullest observations about Jesus possible.

In reality, we have no indication from the text that he's even glad to be there. Or perhaps he is perfectly happy to be part of the celebration, but at the very least he at first seems reluctant to get involved in the reception planning. I remember being at a friend's wedding reception when the punch ran out. People were getting grumpy, and this included the helpless bystanders who were "volunteered" into solving the problem. In any event, we don't see Jesus at this party "living it up." There is no lampshade on his head.

And yet, wherever Jesus goes, happy or angry, he is always the life of the party.

He cannot help changing the climate of any room. His very presence electrifies the atmosphere. The spirit of any space always adjusts to his demeanor, and not vice versa. And in this instance, his "manifested glory" enhances the occasion.

Jesus could very easily provide some watered-down drink. Hosts always save the poor wine for last (v. 10). Or he could provide them nothing at all. But one thing Jesus cannot do is mediocrity. If it is wine you must have, he figures, you must have the finest vintage. Jesus always brings the good stuff.

But the exchange with his mother prior to the miracle is curious. Is he not planning to manifest his glory at this time? Is he

coerced? Does he jump the gun on his ministerial debut? His response to her request for assistance prompts us to go deeper than
the silly "Jesus the party animal" trope.

## Mama Said "Knock You Out"

Mary makes the wedding's problem Jesus's problem. Jesus replies:
"Woman, what does this have to do with me? My hour has not yet
come" (v. 4). In the original context, Jesus referring to his mother
as "woman" is not quite as rude as it sounds to our modern ears,
and yet, no matter how you slice it, these are hard words.

John Calvin says the Son is not rebuking his mother so much
as making it explicit that his mother is not his commander: "[S]he
was not sinning knowingly and willingly," he writes, "but Christ
just meets the danger of his mother's words being misconstrued, as
if it were at her behest that he afterwards performed the miracle."[3]

This is likely true. From his adolescence (Luke 2:49) till well
into his ministry (Matt. 12:48), Jesus repeatedly finds it necessary
to assert the primacy of his heavenly Father over his earthly family.
Jesus loves his mother very much. He is an excellent Son. But he
will not be a mama's boy. Mary will not be the boss of him.

But depths remain to be explored in this exchange. If Jesus is
making it clear that he's no one's magic trick, what specific resonance might this disavowal to his own mother have for the wedding
party? For Jesus's mission field? For us today? John Piper helpfully
probes:

> [H]e could have said very gently, "Yes, Mother, I know. I'll
> take care of it immediately." That's what he did, but that's not
> what he said. That makes us ask why he spoke to her this way.
> If you are going to do what your mother has in mind anyway,
> why don't you simply agree with her and then do it? Why the
> off-putting words?
>
> I think the answer is that Jesus felt a burden to make
> clear not only to his mother and his brothers and sisters, but

[3] John Calvin, *John* (Wheaton, IL: Crossway, 1994), 50.

to all the rest of us, that because of who he was, physical relationships on earth would not control him or oblige him. His
mother and his physical family would have no special advantage to guide his ministry. And his mother and physical family
would have no special advantage to receive his salvation. . . .

In other words, followers, not family, have a saving relationship with Jesus.

This is what we are seeing in John 2:4. "They have no
wine. . . ." "Woman, what does this have to do with me?"
(John 2:3–4). Your relationship with me as mother has no special weight here. You are a woman like every other woman.
My Father in heaven, not any human being, determines what
miracles I perform. And the pathway into my favor is faith,
not family.

This is very good news for us. It doesn't matter what family line we come from. Your parents may be the most ungodly
people you know. That will not keep you from the favor of
Jesus. Faith, not family, makes you his friend.[4]

This is a good exposition because it takes us right to the substance of the gospel, helping us see the glory manifested by Jesus
in this miracle event, even before the miracle is performed! By reminding Mary of the limits of her dominion over his behavior, he
is reminding us of the limits of his dominion over salvation, or,
rather, the lack thereof. Jesus will not be beholden to his family,
be it biological or ethnic, and neither will his kingdom. As Piper
writes, "The pathway into [his] favor is faith." The disciples trace
this line (John 2:11). Thus, his rebuke of his mother is a good word
for us, because it means that our inheritance in grace is not contingent upon our family ties, race, ethnicity, social status, or any other
arbitrary earthly thing, but instead upon the favor of God himself. It
is our faith that is credited to us as righteousness, not our pedigree.

There is something else, though, in Jesus's response to his

---

[4] John Piper, "Obedient Son, Ultimate Purifier, All-Providing Bridegroom," sermon, Bethlehem Baptist Church, Minneapolis, MN (December 14, 2008), www.desiringgod.org/resource-library/sermons/obedient
-son-ultimate-purifier-all-providing-bridegroom.

mother, something that encapsulates rhetorically a significant occurrence theologically. He says to her, "My hour has not yet come" (v. 4). This cannot mean, as some may suppose, that it is not his time to "debut," because he does precisely that. No, when Jesus refers to "my hour" or "my time," he typically refers to one of two things: the time to commence going to the cross or the full revelation of his transcendent glory.[5] This is neither of those moments, but it is a decisive moment nevertheless. And we should envision that word *nevertheless* as marking the shift from Jesus's response to his mother in word and Jesus's response to his mother in deed. Essentially, what transpires subsequently can be paraphrased like this: "Mother, it is not the time to fully unveil my redemptive purpose in the world. Nevertheless, I will provide a partial service at present that points to that fullness in the future."

Mary obediently submits to her Son, then, stepping aside to entrust the party to his miraculous power—although we have no textual indication this is even what she's requesting from him—or his clever resourcefulness. "Do whatever he says," she tells the servants. "My Son will take care of it." And he does.

Jesus loves his mother. He wants to please her. He knows she's asking for more than she realizes. But very often Jesus is eager to give those who submit to his authority more than they could ask or imagine (Eph. 3:20; John 1:16). The event that follows reveals a subtle reflection of the truth of the incarnation, Jesus showing himself as both Mary's sovereign Lord and her obedient Son.

There is more glory to be seen in the miracle, however. Mary wants her Son to save the wedding host from the scandal of running out of wine, and Jesus uses the opportunity to signify a salvation that *is* a scandal.

## The Promise Made Present

"Now there were six stone water jars there for the Jewish rites of purification, each holding twenty or thirty gallons" (John 2:6). Do

---

[5] See Carson, *The Gospel according to John*, 172.

you suppose that the jars Jesus uses are connected to Jewish religious rites by happenstance? Craig Blomberg tells us bluntly that this miracle is a "vivid illustration of the transformation of the old 'water' of Mosaic religion into the new 'wine' of the kingdom"[6]

Jesus later gives a teaching on weddings and wine (and its containers) that serves as an important explication of what is taking place in this miracle:

> And Jesus said to them, "Can the wedding guests fast while the bridegroom is with them? As long as they have the bridegroom with them, they cannot fast. The days will come when the bridegroom is taken away from them, and then they will fast in that day. No one sews a piece of unshrunk cloth on an old garment. If he does, the patch tears away from it, the new from the old, and a worse tear is made. And no one puts new wine into old wineskins. If he does, the wine will burst the skins—and the wine is destroyed, and so are the skins. But new wine is for fresh wineskins." (Mark 2:19–22)

All along his way inaugurating the new covenant, Jesus is ushering in the new creation. The wine of the old covenant is maintained well enough in the old structures—the temple system with its sacrifices and rituals. But the wine of the new covenant needs newness. The presence of God, once localized in the Most Holy Place, is now on foot. He will soon be present everywhere in Spirit, dwelling in his people, whose bodies are each the temple (1 Cor. 6:19) and in the midst of whom is the kingdom (Luke 17:21).

The old way is defunct, expired, kaput. "You can fill up your jars to brimming with the water of your old-time religion," Jesus says, "and I will replace it with the new wine of the gospel." In doing this, Jesus is not inventing something new, but simply presenting what has been promised in the old religion itself.

Wine throughout the Old Testament has a variegated resonance. Wine represents joy (Ps. 104:15; Eccl. 10:19), victory (Isa. 62:8–9),

---

[6] Blomberg, "The Miracles as Parables," 335.

vindication (Hos. 14:7), satisfaction (Joel 2:19), abundance (Joel 2:24; 3:18), and restoration (Amos 9:13–14). In Isaiah 55:1, we find this foretaste of free grace:

> Come, everyone who thirsts,
> come to the waters;
> and he who has no money,
> come, buy and eat!
> Come, buy wine and milk
> without money and without price.

Something for nothing? That is the exchange offered in the gospel of Jesus. Bring your nothingness, and he will give you his everything. It's the only exchange Christ will make. Should we seek to fill our spiritual piggy banks with the currency of our religious effort—should we fill them to brimming—it would not be merit enough. We proffer the water from our brow. It is the best we can afford. But Jesus brings the good stuff.

All the old covenant freight is loaded into the wine Jesus creates. Everyone knows that the best wine is that which is well aged. So Jesus's new wine has all the depth, potency, and flavor of the best vintage. He proclaims it into existence, but it comes loaded with all the flavor of fine wine aged for years and years. Where once there was water, now there is wine, but it does not come, as it were, from "out of nowhere." It comes from the vast ages of promise and expectation, and is fraught with all the hopes, joys, and exultation of the patriarchs and the prophets. This wine comes from the vault of heaven and is steeped through with all the tannins wrought there.

Jesus is not performing a neat trick. He isn't just supplying a need. He is signaling the immediate presence of the ancient promise. John Pryor says, "It is the wine of the eschaton."[7] The kingdom has come. We see it in this wine, and if we find it appealing to the senses, we are bid to come and partake through repentance

---

[7] John W. Pryor, *John: Evangelist of the Covenant People* (Downers Grove, IL: InterVarsity, 1992), 16.

and belief. We are bid, in fact, to come drink of the wine of Christ himself, imbibing his blood as the source of our very life and surpassing joy. Of this wine, Herman Ridderbos writes, "For *now* there is wine as plentiful as water, indeed as plentiful as all the water of purification, which has flowed continually but cannot take away the sin of the world."[8]

And yet, in this moment of festivity, Jesus's hour has not come. Even this provision of abundance is just a foretaste. (It is just like Jesus to make a feast an appetizer.) There is much more to come. In the miracle at Cana, we receive a micro view of the inauguration of God's kingdom through Christ. Witnessing the water transformed to wine begs us to press still further into the greater manifestation of Christ's glory. For at Cana, we see through a glass darkly. But when we are face to face? J. C. Ryle reflects:

> Happy are those who, like the disciples, believe on Him by whom this miracle was wrought. A greater marriage feast than that of Cana will one day be held, when Christ Himself will be the bridegroom and believers will be the bride. A greater glory will one day be manifested, when Jesus shall take to Himself His great power and reign. Blessed will they be in that day who are called to the marriage supper of the Lamb! (Rev. 19:9)[9]

---

[8] Herman N. Ridderbos, *The Gospel According to John: A Theological Commentary*, trans. John Vriend (Grand Rapids, MI: Eerdmans, 1997), 107. Emphasis original.
[9] J. C. Ryle, *Expository Thoughts on the Gospels for Family and Private Use*, vol. 1, St. John (New York: Robert Carter and Brothers, 1879), 91–92.

# 3

# A Trail of Breadcrumbs

In turning water into wine, Jesus shows, among many things, his mastery of nature. If the point is missed there, it surely cannot be missed in Matthew 17:24–27.

In this life, there are two things, we are told, that are inevitable. The first is death, which Jesus both promised (Matt. 10:16–21) and required (Matt. 16:24–25). While you're waiting on that, taxes come due, as this passage shows:

> When they came to Capernaum, the collectors of the two-drachma tax went up to Peter and said, "Does your teacher not pay the tax?" He said, "Yes." And when he came into the house, Jesus spoke to him first, saying, "What do you think, Simon? From whom do kings of the earth take toll or tax? From their sons or from others?" And when he said, "From others," Jesus said to him, "Then the sons are free. However, not to give offense to them, go to the sea and cast a hook and take the first fish that comes up, and when you open its mouth you will find a shekel. Take that and give it to them for me and for yourself."

These four verses hold a wealth of enlightenment, but the first thing I love about this story is that Jesus knows what is on Peter's mind when he enters the house. Jesus's omniscience is on display. It gets better, but first comes the convoluted stuff. Jesus wants to talk tax law with Peter. "Do the sons of kings pay taxes?" Of course not. The theological implication hangs there in the air, shining like a freshly minted gold piece.

The two-drachma tax is meant for the temple, the temple is owned by God, and Jesus is the Son of God; therefore, Jesus should not be obligated to pay this tax. He is exempt on the basis of his familial relationship with the temple's rightful owner. Indeed, Jesus himself on numerous occasions walks into the temple and acts like he owns the place! But in a concession similar to the one made at the wedding in Cana, Jesus forgoes his exemption and agrees to pay the tax. Just as he made it clear in fulfilling his mother's wishes that he was not beholden to her, he fulfills the wishes of the tax collectors while clarifying his lack of obligation.

This is a picture of grace. Jesus owes us nothing. This is clear from the message of the gospel itself, through which Jesus gives us everything.

But the thing required is money, and Jesus has had lots of difficult things to say about money, about accumulating it (Matt. 19:23; Luke 6:24) and about stewarding it (Mark 12:17, 43–44; Luke 14:13), and so it is perhaps spiritually significant that he sends Peter to the sea to fetch payment for his two-drachma tax. One of the points of putting the shekel in the maw of a fish may be Jesus's reluctance to be seen as a provider of financial riches. Contrary to what we hear from so many prosperity preachers, Jesus does not exist to be our personal ATM. "If it's money you want—taxes even, for the corrupt system that is passing away—you won't get it from my fingers," he seems to be saying.

But in all of that, there is still this: from a great distance, Jesus predicts and causes the appearance of the right coin in the right fish drawn up by the right man at the right time. In this instance, perhaps, the most obvious point of the story is the most powerful! As St. Jerome says of this incident, "I know not which to admire most here, our Lord's foreknowledge or His greatness."[1]

---

[1] St. Jerome, quoted in J. Ligon Duncan, "The King's Son Pays the Tax," sermon, First Presbyterian Church, Jackson, Mississippi (n.d.), http://www.fpcjackson.org/resources/sermons/matthew/matthew_vol_5-6/39 amatt.htm.

Jesus is master of money and of mouths. After his resurrection, he provides fish again, instructing the disciples on just where to cast their nets to produce a catch so large they can't haul it into the boat (John 21:4–6). This act bears the hallmarks of Christ's playful side—I can picture him smirking as he gives the instructions, then laughing when, after the haul, they shout in realization, "It is the Lord!" (v. 7). Provision is one of Jesus's favorite things to make, provision of food especially.

The most famous miraculous provision, of course, is recorded in John 6, where we read that Jesus takes five pieces of bread and two fishes from a boy's lunch box and turns it into a meal for five thousand. A lot has been written on John 6; it is a beautiful chapter. Some look to the text as an example of Jesus's providing felt needs to gather a crowd, to reach people. Like the conclusion often drawn from the wedding miracle that "Jesus likes to party," this sort of summation is worthy of a thousand yawns. It's not that it isn't true, only that it's remarkably shortsighted. John 6 shows Jesus's utter willingness to confound and disturb the same crowd he's gathered. He knows, even if many evangelical churches do not, that what you win them with is what you win them to:

> "I am the bread of life. Your fathers ate the manna in the wilderness, and they died. This is the bread that comes down from heaven, so that one may eat of it and not die. I am the living bread that came down from heaven. If anyone eats of this bread, he will live forever. And the bread that I will give for the life of the world is my flesh."
>
> The Jews then disputed among themselves, saying, "How can this man give us his flesh to eat?" So Jesus said to them, "Truly, truly, I say to you, unless you eat the flesh of the Son of Man and drink his blood, you have no life in you. Whoever feeds on my flesh and drinks my blood has eternal life, and I will raise him up on the last day. For my flesh is true food, and my blood is true drink." (John 6:48–55)

There is an obvious difference between the provision of the

meal in John 6 and the provision of the temple tax in Matthew 17. In the former, Jesus manifests multiplied fish and loaves from his hands. In the latter, Jesus manifests the coin from a distance. But aside from the sheer divine power evidenced in both miracles, there is a significant similarity. In Matthew 17, Peter has to follow the path Jesus lays out for him to find what is needed. And this is no less true in John 6. Jesus warns his disciples not to fixate on the miracle but to trace its arc back to the miracle worker. He wants his disciples to follow the miraculous provision, like a trail of bread-crumbs, to the bread of life.

## The Less Famous but Just as Miraculous Feeding of the Four Thousand

We turn now to a less obvious text in Mark 8, where Jesus works another miraculous provision. Mark's treatment of the feeding of the four thousand is less complex than John's of the feeding of the five thousand (which Mark also records in 6:30–44), and it is shorter, too. And while John 6 is punctuated with warnings to the miracle witnesses, the warning in Mark 8 is more direct and, in some ways, more personally placed. The story begins this way:

> In those days, when again a great crowd had gathered, and they had nothing to eat, he called his disciples to him and said to them, "I have compassion on the crowd, because they have been with me now three days and have nothing to eat. And if I send them away hungry to their homes, they will faint on the way. And some of them have come from far away." And his disciples answered him, "How can one feed these people with bread here in this desolate place?" And he asked them, "How many loaves do you have?" They said, "Seven." And he directed the crowd to sit down on the ground. And he took the seven loaves, and having given thanks, he broke them and gave them to his disciples to set before the people; and they set them before the crowd. And they had a few small fish. And having blessed them, he said that these also should be set be-

fore them. And they ate and were satisfied. And they took up the broken pieces left over, seven baskets full. (Mark 8:1–8)

One of the first things we notice is Jesus's disposition toward the crowd. He has great compassion for them. But we also see his disposition about the situation, about the apparent dilemma. Is Jesus worried about how the crowd will be fed? Is Jesus acting as if he is at a loss as to how to provide for them?

Assessing the need, our Lord turns the situation into a teachable moment for his disciples. He wants the disciples to have his view. "See what I see," he's saying between the lines. "Know what I know." Similarly, our Lord wants his church today to confront the apparent desolation of the culture, the apparently dire need of the world this way. He wants the church to have his view, to see as he sees.

The disciples, as usual, do not see the presence of their Lord as much consolation. "How can one feed these people with bread here in this desolate place?" they ask (v. 4). So, remember the feeding of the five thousand? Well, the disciples apparently don't. And in Mark's narrative, it was just two chapters ago! It doesn't even occur to them to see the distinct advantage of a smaller crowd (roughly one thousand less) and more numerous loaves (an additional two). The mouths are fewer and the raw material is greater, but the disciples are just as thickheaded as ever (it gets worse later). Like us, the disciples are stupid and forgetful at the same time.

Jesus once again blesses the small provision of fish and loaves, and supplies the needs of four thousand hungry people, who all eat until they are satisfied (v. 8). Once again, against all odds, Jesus can be trusted with very little to satisfy very much.

And he doesn't just satisfy; he *more than* satisfies. As with the feeding of the five thousand, there are plenty of leftovers for the doggie bags. Jesus gets carried away with his provision, reminding us again that when it comes to the provision of Christ himself, we are not marginally satisfied—steadying the rumble in our tummies—but joyously full! In Christ, we are eternally satisfied, abundantly satisfied, mightily satisfied. And because the miracles are not ends in themselves but signs pointing to Jesus himself, we are reminded here that we are not merely saved but eternally saved, abundantly saved, mightily saved.

Through the gospel, let us remember, we are satisfied with seven baskets besides: regeneration, pardon, justification, adoption, union, sanctification, and glorification—and still more. His mercies, like the bread of heaven sent to the children of Israel, are new every morning.

Jesus sends four thousand people away (v. 9), but he sends them away full. That is what Jesus always does when we come to him hungry.

In Mark 8, he once again demonstrates his divine authority over creation in order to testify to the awesome provision of eternal life in the new creation.

## Further Adventures in Missing the Point

In Exodus 16, we learn that just forty-five days after God had orchestrated the deliverance of the children of Israel from the bondage of Egypt via supernatural plagues, strategic afflictions, cosmic signs, creeping death, the guiding visions of pillars of cloud and fire, and the miraculous parting of a sea, followed shortly thereafter by the miraculous sweetening of bitter water to their taste, the Israelites were whining about their hunger:

> Would that we had died by the hand of the LORD in the land of Egypt, when we sat by the meat pots and ate bread to the full, for you have brought us out into this wilderness to kill this whole assembly with hunger. (v. 3)

Oh, brother. Somebody call the "waaambulance."

That's what we say, with the benefit of exegetical superiority. It's easy to project when we disassociate. But that's not what the Lord says, and it's not what he says to us, even when our faithless grumbling calls forth the ages-old echo of Exodus. The Lord says this: "Behold, I am about to rain bread from heaven for you" (v. 4).

This promise of gracious provision comes with some constraints, however, which the Israelites predictably break. In Exodus 17, they resume their quarreling with God, and he graciously turns their whine into water by instructing Moses to strike a rock.

The entire book of Exodus, if titled after the disposition of the Israelites, might be called "Further Adventures in Missing the Point."

But them is us. And it's easy to forget this reality even in the New Testament, as we frequently scoff at the Pharisees and snicker at the disciples. We are no more virtuous in intellect or memory than they. In our flesh, today as then, the life of discipleship could be summarized with the question "What have you done for me *lately*?"

Flash forward to the walking around days of the rock (Acts 4:11) who is the water (John 4:14). The grumbling and testing cannot be escaped. Continuing in Mark 8:

> And immediately he got into the boat with his disciples and went to the district of Dalmanutha. The Pharisees came and began to argue with him, seeking from him a sign from heaven to test him. (vv. 10–11)

What's interesting about this request is that they want Jesus to work a wonder, and he literally has just done that. And the very fact that Jesus has replicated a miraculous feeding of thousands of people proves it isn't some serendipitous fluke. The same is true of the many healings Jesus performs. That he can perform them seemingly at will proves he is not simply a vehicle for some force (although that is true on some level, as the Son submitted to the Father and relied on the Spirit) but that he is the very force itself.

But there's a difference between requesting and testing. There's a difference between asking and demanding. The fact that the Pharisees come "to argue with him" shows what kind of seeking they are doing. The problem is that when you seek signs instead of the signified, you're always a day late and a miracle short.

Jesus's miracles are but the means of his self-disclosure, not the purpose of it.

> And he sighed deeply in his spirit and said, "Why does this generation seek a sign? Truly, I say to you, no sign will be given to this generation." (v. 12)

This is a sigh of frustration. A deep sigh. It carries with it the knowledge that Jesus has come as a Jew to the Jews, as a son of David to the children of Israel, as the Messiah of this nation to these people, and the very people who should know who he is—the religious shepherds of the nation, the scholars of the Torah, the practitioners of the rites he is regularly fulfilling and surpassing—are utterly and totally blind to him. The experts are expertly blowing it. There is a parallel of this exchange in Matthew's Gospel, when the leaders come pestering for a wonder:

> Then some of the scribes and Pharisees answered him, saying, "Teacher, we wish to see a sign from you." But he answered them, "An evil and adulterous generation seeks for a sign, but no sign will be given to it except the sign of the prophet Jonah. For just as Jonah was three days and three nights in the belly of the great fish, so will the Son of Man be three days and three nights in the heart of the earth." (Matt. 12:38–40)

Jesus even has the mercy to translate the impending sign of Jonah for them, making it as clear as appropriate in the moment that unless they believe in his coming death and resurrection, all the miracles leading up to it will merit them nothing.

He makes no bones about it: if you're looking for signs, you're going to miss out on salvation. No sign will be given the hard in heart but Jesus himself. No sign will wake you from your stupor but Jesus himself.

We see this vividly in effect in Jesus's parable of the rich man and Lazarus (Luke 16:19–31). From the torment of Hades, the rich man begs Abraham to send someone from the dead to his family so they will believe. Abraham tells him that if they don't believe Moses and the Prophets, they won't be convinced by a miracle.

It seems an odd thing to say, since every good Jew would claim to believe Moses and the Prophets, but the point, in light of the new covenant's dawning, is that true belief in Moses and the Prophets results in true belief in Christ. The Law and the Prophets testify to Jesus (Mark 9:4–8; Luke 24:27).

The world is always looking for a sign. We all claim to want a miracle. "Seeing is believing," we insist. But what we really want is a miracle *drug*—something that ignores our shame, fulfills our dreams, and gives us meaning and purpose in life, all accompanied by great pleasure, of course.

As the church exists to be on mission with Jesus to seek and save the lost, we have essentially three options to offer them: religiosity, worldliness, or Jesus. Only one of those three actually saves men. What we offer directly results from how we view those in need—with the powerful compassion of Christ or the clueless exasperation of the flesh—and what we see their need to be. Should we provide bread and water? Of course. But man will not live on bread alone (Matt. 4:4). That is the whole point of the trajectory of John 6 and, if we have the eyes to see, of Mark 8:1–21.

Jesus, who graciously condescends to grant us miracles such as the breath of life every day, cannot be pestered into honoring our self-exalted skepticism with the disembodied signs we keep yammering for. "You don't need signs," he's saying, "you need me." To clamor for miracles is to scurry about for crumbs.

As St. Augustine says: "You ask for your reward and the Giver is himself the gift. What more can you want?"[2]

## Grace for the Stupid

My friend Ray Ortlund pastors Immanuel Church in Nashville, Tennessee, where they rehearse what they call "The Immanuel Mantra." This mantra consists of three basic parts, as follows:

---

[2] Augustine, *Daily Readings with St. Augustine*, ed. Dame Maura Sée (Springfield, IL: Templegate, 1987), 25.

I am a complete idiot.

My future is incredibly bright.

Anyone can get in on this.[3]

One of the most beautiful entailments of the good news of Jesus Christ is that receiving it is not contingent upon our ability to "get it." In actuality, the power of the gospel presupposes our total inability to get it (1 Cor. 2:14). In this way, the wisdom of the world is made foolish (1 Cor. 1:20). In the words of the prophet, "The wise men shall be put to shame; they shall be dismayed and taken; behold, they have rejected the word of the LORD, so what wisdom is in them?" (Jer. 8:9). Salvation, from top to bottom, is all of grace. This is good news for us idiots. To wit:

> And he left them, got into the boat again, and went to the other side.
> Now they had forgotten to bring bread, and they had only one loaf with them in the boat. And he cautioned them, saying, "Watch out; beware of the leaven of the Pharisees and the leaven of Herod." (Mark 8:13–15)

Jesus turns his unfortunate encounter with the Pharisees into a teachable moment for his disciples. The way of the world offers two kinds of wisdom, and though they each essentially grow from the same root sin of pride, they manifest in disparate ways. The leaven of the Pharisees is their teaching, according to the parallel in Matthew 16:12, that is puffed up and outwardly righteous while inwardly corrupt and rotten. That way lies religiosity, religion for religion's sake. The leaven of Herod, on the other hand, is worldliness.

In our spiritual ignorance, we often think the solution to either one is the other. All those who dabble in religiosity need is a good

---

[3] You can watch Dr. Ortlund elaborate on the mantra at https://vimeo.com/59326626.

dose of worldly fun. They just need to loosen up, get a little dirty. And, of course, the worldly sorts really need to straighten up and get their act together. This is the primary message of the gospel-deficient church: "Behave!"

But as appealing as both approaches can be, both are fundamentally a rejection of Jesus. And the answer to both is Jesus.

Because they do not derive from the centrality of Jesus and the finding of him as all-satisfying and ever-glorious, both the leaven of the Pharisees (religiosity) and the leaven of Herod (worldliness) are profoundly and devastatingly stupid.

This is Jesus's message to his followers here: "Wake up! Keep a lookout. Beware of these viewpoints. If you give them an inch, they will take a mile. Just as a little leaven infiltrates the whole lump, a dash of legalism or a dash of license can corrupt your faith."

Jesus is expressly talking about spiritual matters. And this is the response of the disciples: "[T]hey began discussing with one another the fact that they had no bread" (Mark 8:16).

Say the mantra with me now: "I am a complete idiot."

Jesus has just dropped some critical knowledge on them, and what do they do? They worry about not having bread. *Again.*

Days after Jesus miraculously feeds the five thousand, they are stumped as to how they might provide for four thousand, and hours after he miraculously feeds the four thousand, they can't for the life of them figure out how they might get their twelve bellies full.

> And Jesus, aware of this, said to them, "Why are you discussing the fact that you have no bread? Do you not yet perceive or understand? Are your hearts hardened? Having eyes do you not see, and having ears do you not hear? And do you not remember? When I broke the five loaves for the five thousand, how many baskets full of broken pieces did you take up?" They said to him, "Twelve." "And the seven for the four thousand, how many baskets full of broken pieces did you take up?" And they said to him, "Seven." And he said to them, "Do you not yet understand?" (vv. 17–21)

Hey, stupids, you have the giver of life with you!

We do this, too. We are forgetful of God's enormous, miraculous provision of himself each and every day. Like the Israelites fresh out of Egypt, having been made spiritual witnesses to the glory of Christ, who has set us eternally free, clothed us in his righteousness, and granted to us the divine right of immortality, we murmur in so many of our prayers, "You have brought us out here to kill us with hunger!"

The DNA for this dumbness began in the garden, embedded in the fall. Adam and Eve looked at the tree, listened to the Serpent, and decided that God doesn't really satisfy. They doubted all the way to disbelief.

Yet Christ brings us to desolate places specifically to rid our visions of anything alluring but himself. This is why the DNA of this stupidity comes from the garden but the genetic reengineering of wisdom comes from the desert.

In Matthew 4:1–11, Jesus is led into the wilderness to be tempted by the Devil, first with that bread we're always hungering for. And Jesus is certainly hungry. But his eyes are not on signs but on the signified. Second, then, the Devil tells the Lord to throw himself off the temple and into the arms of the angels. Is this religious self-interest not the leaven of the Pharisees? Jesus, wary of this leaven, refuses. So the tempter offers Jesus the world, the leaven of Herod. And where Adam and Eve failed, Christ succeeds. He does not use the world's wisdom to persevere, for if he did, he would certainly stuff his face, take the plunge, and seek the greedy gain. Instead, the embodiment of wisdom walks by faith and puts wickedness to shame.

And he does all of this to save his stupid friends who cannot see it to do it themselves. It is for this reason that Paul begins his great gospel proclamation in 1 Corinthians 15 with, "Now *I would remind you*, brothers, of the gospel I preached to you" (v. 1).

Do you not yet understand? Is your heart hard?

Jesus is specializing in complete idiots! He specifically prefers them. The future of those yahoos in the boat scratching their heads about the forgotten bread is, despite themselves, incredibly bright.

And because Jesus specializes in enlightening the foolish and strengthening the weak, anyone can get in on this.

If you look to Jesus, the bread of life, and ask him to satisfy your hunger, he will not give you a stone. He will give you himself. Let us then stop begging for signs and start beholding Jesus.

There is one great sign that you are loved more than you thought. It is the cross. And there is a still further sign that you will live in this love forever. It is the empty tomb.

Come, you who hunger, bring your nothingness and trade it for the abundant wine and bread of Jesus Christ.

## 4

# Walking Around Like He Made the Place

I once received an e-mail from a fellow who said he felt that God had been unusually hard on him. Specifically, he said he felt like a dog on a leash who had gone beyond respect for his master into the realm of fear of the next lash. He said he told God in his prayers that he wouldn't treat his own son the way God was treating him.

Do you ever feel that way? Do you feel as though God is up in heaven, manipulating you like a sadistic puppet master, pulling your strings and putting you through hell for no good reason?

The 1998 film *The Truman Show* tells the story of Truman Burbank, a mild-mannered insurance adjuster living with his pleasant wife in a pleasant home in a pleasant island village called Seahaven. Truman's entire life can be described as quaint. He has everything he needs conveniently around him in his picture-perfect community. He basically lives in a postcard.

But something inside of Truman longs to get away. He dreams wistfully of exploring the world. But there is one problem: he has a crippling fear of open water that has kept him for his entire life on the island of Seahaven. He cannot bring himself to board a boat or even cross a bridge. Still, his longing to explore will not diminish.

One day, as Truman is on his way to work, a strange metallic object falls from the sky and crashes next to him. A radio broadcast later explains that a plane has dropped parts over the town, but Truman is still unsettled. He eventually encounters more strange phenomena. A frequency on the radio dial broadcasts what sounds like a voice narrating his every move. An open elevator shaft in a building downtown reveals no elevator but what looks like a theater's backstage area. Truman sits in his car in his driveway for long periods of time and discovers that the traffic in the neighborhood appears to be on a loop, the same vehicles and pedestrians passing the same places according to some unknown pattern.

What does it all mean?

Truman eventually discovers that his entire life is false. From birth, he has unwittingly been the subject of a television program. In an equal parts perverse and brilliant experiment, his life has become the longest running, round-the-clock reality show. All of the people in his life, including his parents and his wife—indeed, all the citizens of the town of Seahaven—are actors. And the very island itself is a complex and vast set, all residing underneath an imperceptible dome.

But Truman has seen enough. He does not want to be the star of anyone's voyeurism, so he conspires to escape the show and eventually finds himself, despite his deepest fears, jumping into a sailboat and braving the open water of the sea.

On and on he sails, as far as the world may take him.

But this world is false, controlled by a master manipulator named Christof (oddly enough), who is the genius behind the show and its director and producer. From his booth in the heavens, Christof controls the wind, rain, and ocean in the set, and he whips up a perilous storm. It makes for edge-of-your-seat television, but the risk to Truman is very real. Millions of viewers around the world watched his birth, and now they may actually witness his death.

Still Truman sails, tossed about like a rag doll on the small vessel, until he is knocked unconscious and becomes dangerously lashed to the boat. Eventually, however, the prow crashes through the wall at the end of the experimental world. Truman trium-phantly bids his puppet master adieu for good.

It's a powerful scene in a powerful movie, and my hunch is that many who watch the entire story play out resonate with some of the elements of the tale on a spiritual level. No, very few of us will ever be the stars of television shows, knowingly or unknowingly, but very many of us might see in Truman's story a resemblance to our relationships with God.

"If God is up there," many think, "he has a lot of explaining to do. I feel like I just exist to be knocked around for his entertain-ment. If I could, I would just check out of this world and break out of these abusive confines."

*The Truman Show* strikes a serious theological chord. But as it pertains to the biblical gospel, it falls short on one serious level. In the biblical story, the director is not simply up in the heavens, pushing buttons and pulling levers on our tumultuous journey; he is in the boat.

## Asleep at the Wheel

By the time the disciples get into their boat with Jesus in Mark 4, they have already seen and heard plenty enough to bolster their faith. In Mark's chronology, they have witnessed multiple heal-ings, many exorcisms, and even the uncommonly powerful author-ity with which Jesus preaches. After one particularly long day of preaching, Jesus is ready to take a break, so they board a vessel to cross the Sea of Galilee. On the way over, our Lord falls asleep. The story that ensues is frequently called "Jesus Calms the Storm." I love that William Hendriksen in his commentary titles this pas-sage "A Tempest Stilled,"[1] which could refer as easily to the God of the universe dozing on his pillow as to the storm he commands.

This incident is chronicled in all three Synoptic Gospels, but Mark's, the shortest of the three, actually contains a (slightly) more detailed account. We find this version in Mark 4:35–41:

---

[1] William Hendriksen, *The Gospel of Mark* (Grand Rapids, MI: Baker, 1990), 175.

On that day, when evening had come, he said to them, "Let us go across to the other side." And leaving the crowd, they took him with them in the boat, just as he was. And other boats were with him. And a great windstorm arose, and the waves were breaking into the boat, so that the boat was already fill-ing. But he was in the stern, asleep on the cushion. And they woke him and said to him, "Teacher, do you not care that we are perishing?" And he awoke and rebuked the wind and said to the sea, "Peace! Be still!" And the wind ceased, and there was a great calm. He said to them, "Why are you so afraid? Have you still no faith?" And they were filled with great fear and said to one another, "Who then is this, that even the wind and the sea obey him?"

In this passage, we see evidence of the incarnation. Within seven verses, Jesus is both sleeping from human weariness and speaking from divine authority. The former we can certainly un-derstand. We know tiredness. But pastors who preach for long periods of time might feel the weariness in this text with extra resonance.

I don't know how some of my ministry friends do it, juggling multiple services on a weekend, giving it all they've got each time, while still making themselves available to meet and counsel with people between sermons. I typically preach once a weekend, and when I execute my task honorably, it is surprisingly draining. It may not look like much to stand up and yell at people for thirty to forty-five minutes—okay, I'll be honest, for forty-five minutes to an hour. But there is something I can only describe as a "psychic weight" to the act of preaching by a preacher who is conscious of taking with him into the pulpit the mantle of the gospel, the eternal stakes of spiritual power, to deliver faithfully the Word of God and give its sense (Neh. 8:8).

I have preached a few conference events that consisted of four or five hour-long sessions with only short breaks between them. Usually by the end, I don't remember my own name and need to go night-night. But I know men who regularly preach for much longer, and I'm in awe of them.

But Jesus blows all of us sissy preachers out of the water. He preaches for long periods of time, in the heat of the outdoors, usually accompanied by thoughtless and incompetent assistants, without the benefit of a green room or refrigerated bottled water, followed frequently by personal, deep engagements with countless needy people, many of whom he heals, restores, or delivers, apparently at the expense of more power (if Luke 8:46 is any indication), and often has to follow it all with tiresome debriefings with his disciples, where he ends up having to re-teach and re-explain most of the day's events to make sure they understand. And then, to top it all off, he apparently has no bed of his own to return to at night (Matt. 8:20)!

It is no wonder that Jesus often withdraws to lonely places to pray (Luke 5:16) and, I assume, to catch his breath and (as they say) "recharge his batteries." And it is no wonder that at the end of another apparently grueling day of real up-close-and-personal ministry, Jesus is tired and needs a nap:

> And a great windstorm arose, and the waves were breaking into the boat, so that the boat was already filling. But he was in the stern, asleep on the cushion. (Mark 4:37–38a)

Asleep! How dare he?

Jesus is able to sleep during the storm that develops because he's very, very tired. But Jesus is also able to sleep during the storm because he's very, very much in control. He may be lying down in the back of the boat with his eyes closed, but he is also firmly at the wheel. The disciples' snoring Sovereign is snoring *because* he is sovereign.

Our incarnate Lord has skin you can pierce—but only if he lets you (Luke 4:29–30; John 10:17–18).

In fact, we get no sense from any passage in any of the Gospels that Jesus Christ is ever *not* in control—not even during his arrest, torture, and crucifixion. Everything that happens to him, he goes to willingly. He has submitted himself to the will of his heavenly Father, and this submission has entailed coming to the world not as its condemner but as its servant. He has emptied himself, not seeing his equality with the Father as something to be exploited or leveraged. On his way to the cross, he has not jumped through the divine loophole or pulled the heavenly parachute. But he is never, ever out of control—not even when he's sleeping.

## Jesus RSVPs the Pity Party

Mark continues: "And they woke him and said to him, 'Teacher, do you not care that we are perishing?'" (Mark 4:38b).

It is easy to ridicule the disciples at this point, to see them in some sense as being quite dramatic. But the text does not tell us the ride is bumpy. It tells us that the boat is filling with water from the waves. If it were you or I in that boat, even if Jesus were in the flesh with us, nine times out of ten fear would trump theology. In a situation like the one described, terror is practically instinctual. In the middle of a raucous storm, boat taking on water, "We're all gonna die!" is not a punch line. It's a valid prediction.

And yet, Jesus is sleeping. Like the disciples, I can't get over this. How tired do you have to be to sleep through getting knocked about in the stern of a jostling boat, getting water sloshed on you from the rising level in the bilge, let alone thunder and the frantic shouting of your friends? There is, in a way, something quite comic about this passage. And it makes the disciples' question sort of humorous. I assume there is a level of anger in it, a smidgen of sarcasm added to the terror: "Don't you care that we're dying?"

Does that sound at all like any of your prayers? Does it at all resemble your theology these days? "This stuff must be happening because God doesn't care about me."

The cry of the disciples is as common as the human heart. Their question evinces two great temptations we face in the midst of any difficulty.

First, we are often tempted in trouble to equate worry with concern. Just as the disciples leap to conclusions about Jesus's sleeping, you and I tend to get very frustrated when others refuse to get infected with our anxiety. I've counseled quite a few married couples, for instance, who have wandered into a communication standoff in part because the wife has mistaken her husband's failure to mirror her nervousness as failure to care about the issues involved. Sometimes explaining the different ways men and women tend to process information and deal with stress helps to clear the air, as does encouraging husbands to be more vocal about their thoughts and feelings with their wives. But very often the essential breakdown comes from logic like this: "This is a very big deal. That's why I'm freaking out about it. You must not think it's a very big deal because you're not freaking out."

The reality is that sometimes people share our concern without sharing our worry. That's a good thing. And it's quite Christlike. Remember that worry is forbidden for the Christian (Matt. 6:25; Phil. 4:6) and that it won't get you anywhere anyway.

And as in Mark 4, Jesus may come to your pity party, but he won't participate. He will sit by you, loving you, caring about you, and overseeing all of your troubles, but he won't for a second share in your anxiety unless you're trying to get rid of it.

There is a reason the most repeated command in the Bible is "Be not afraid."

The second temptation we face when going through enormous difficulty is more directly theological: we tend to assume that a loving God would not let us suffer.

There is perhaps no line of thinking more dangerous, more insidious, and more utterly unchristian than this one. The cry "Do you not care that I'm perishing?" becomes the accusation "I'm perishing and you don't care," which gives way to disavowal: "If there is a God, I don't want anything to do with him. He is cruel."

Where we get the idea that Christianity excludes suffering, I don't rightly know. It likely comes mostly from our flesh, from our prideful idolization of comfort and pleasure. It comes somewhat from just plain ol' crappy doctrine. It certainly does not come from the Bible.

In the story of the man whose house is built on the rock (Matt. 7:24–27), the firm foundation does not keep the storm away. In fact, according to the Scriptures, being a Christian means being willing to take on more suffering than the average person. Not only must we endure the same pains, stresses, and diseases of every other mortal, but we agree to take on the added burden of insults, hardships, and persecutions on account of our faith. Dietrich Bonhoeffer writes:

> The cross is laid on every Christian. The first Christ-suffering which every man must experience is the call to abandon the attachments of this world. It is that dying of the old man which is the result of his encounter with Christ. As we embark upon discipleship we surrender ourselves to Christ in union with his death—we give over our lives to death. Thus it begins; the cross is not the terrible end to an otherwise god-fearing and happy life, but it meets us at the beginning of our communion with Christ. When Christ calls a man, he bids him come and die.[2]

The call to discipleship, in other words, is not an invitation for one of those popular Christian cruises. I can see the advertisement in the Christian magazine now:

> Jesus! Shuffleboard! Seafood Buffet! Join Jesus Christ and twelve other influential teachers for seven luxurious days and six restful nights on the maiden voyage of our five-star, five-story ship of dreams, the S.S. Smooth Sailing. Enjoy karaoke with your favorite psalmists on the lido deck or splash your cares away in our indoor water park with a safe crowd of people who look just like you!

Instead, Jesus calls us into nasty crosswinds in a boat specifi-

---

[2] Dietrich Bonhoeffer, *The Cost of Discipleship* (New York: Macmillan, 1972), 99.

cally designed to make us trust totally in him. And if the boat even appears to offer safety from the waves, Jesus may actually call us *out of it* and into the sea (Matt. 14:29). But in either place, he will be there with us, not to help us worry but to help us believe. Thus, it is imperative that we have our theology straight before we even get in the boat.

Besides *The Truman Show*, one of my other favorite "movies with a boat" is the 1951 John Huston classic *The African Queen*, starring Humphrey Bogart and Katharine Hepburn. The movie takes place in Africa during World War II, and Bogie plays Charlie Allnut, a curmudgeonly boat captain who agrees to transport the missionary Rose, played by Hepburn, down the river from the village of her ministry, which is a German colony, to escape the imminent return of the Nazis. Along the way, they face dangerous animals and dangerous rapids, and *The African Queen* is not a very sturdy boat. To make matters worse, a German gunship is patrolling at the mouth of the river, making escape practically impossible. At one point in their journey, Rose says, "Don't worry, Mr. Allnut," to which the crusty captain replies: "Oh, I ain't worried, Miss. I gave myself up for dead back when we started."

When Christ calls a man into the boat, he bids him give himself up for dead from the start.

### Faith in the Master and Commander

Jesus does care that the disciples are perishing. He may not be worried, but he is not callous:

> And he awoke and rebuked the wind and said to the sea, "Peace! Be still!" And the wind ceased, and there was a great calm. (Mark 4:39)

Herein lies a mighty picture of the sovereignty of Jesus Christ. Hebrews 1:3 says that he sustains the universe by his powerful word. Surely the wind and the sea are but trifles to him. He made them and will remake them. Certainly he can direct them with a word and a wave of his hand.

What is encapsulated in Mark 4:39 is portrayed in a similar adventure in Mark 6:45–52. Tradition tells us that Mark's Gospel was informed by the apostle Peter. It is perhaps indicative of Peter's Christ-formed humility that Mark's account forgoes what Matthew's longer account includes:

> Immediately he made the disciples get into the boat and go before him to the other side, while he dismissed the crowds. And after he had dismissed the crowds, he went up on the mountain by himself to pray. When evening came, he was there alone, but the boat by this time was a long way from the land, beaten by the waves, for the wind was against them. And in the fourth watch of the night he came to them, walking on the sea. But when the disciples saw him walking on the sea, they were terrified, and said, "It is a ghost!" and they cried out in fear. But immediately Jesus spoke to them, saying, "Take heart; it is I. Do not be afraid."
>
> And Peter answered him, "Lord, if it is you, command me to come to you on the water." He said, "Come." So Peter got out of the boat and walked on the water and came to Jesus. But when he saw the wind, he was afraid, and beginning to sink he cried out, "Lord, save me." Jesus immediately reached out his hand and took hold of him, saying to him, "O you of little faith, why did you doubt?" And when they got into the boat, the wind ceased. And those in the boat worshiped him, saying, "Truly you are the Son of God." (Matt. 14:22–33)

In both incidents, Jesus demonstrates his supreme power over nature itself. In Mark's account of the calming of the storm, the same voice that spoke the waters into existence calls out for their tranquility. Hearing the voice of their Creator, the waters obey. In the story of Jesus's walking on the water, we see further his bending the very tumult to his will.

One element in both of these stories not ascertained by the

unstudied reader is this: in the Hebrew mythos, the waters are symbolic of chaos, even evil. This is why the beast is depicted in Revelation 13:1 as coming up out of the sea. (Thus also the references in Isa. 27:1 and Ezek. 32:2.) This is not to say that these accounts in the Gospels are mythical. Neither is it to say that the Jewish people were animists of some kind. It is just that the sea held for them, traditionally and culturally, the specter of untamable wildness, deep darkness, and spiritual chaos. For Jesus to walk around on the water, in other words, is not just an impressive trick. It is a direct proclamation in deed of his authority over the spiritual forces of wickedness in the world. As in the beginning, the Creator God is "separating" order from chaos, conquering the formless void with his sovereign will expressed through his authoritative voice (Gen. 1:2–10).

Even his words of assurance in Matthew 14:27, "It is I," are an implicit declaration of his divine control. The Greek behind the phrase "It is I" is a linguistic echo of the divine name "I AM" presented in the Exodus accounts, themselves no stranger to God's miraculous control of water. Craig Blomberg even points out that the Greek behind the phrase "pass by," used in Mark 6:48 in the account of Jesus walking on the water, is identical to the Septuagint's Exodus 33:19 and 34:6, which recount how God's glory passes by Moses, in which case what is conveyed by "passing by" is a revealing of himself.[3] The Lord's use of "It is I" deserves inclusion, then, in the list of his "I am" statements constituting self-reference to his deity.

Jesus comes walking on the water, declaring in word and deed that he is God. If he is God, he is certainly the master of the seas. And if he is the master of the seas, he is certainly the commander of the seas. "Don't be afraid," he says as he strolls up to the side of the boat, "because it's me."

The statement is paralleled in Mark 4, where Jesus is not outside the boat looking in, but inside the boat *looking into* his disciples:

[3] Craig Blomberg, *Jesus and the Gospels* (Nashville: Broadman and Holman, 1997), 273. See also Jared C. Wilson, *The Storytelling God: Seeing the Glory of Jesus in His Parables* (Wheaton, IL: Crossway, 2014), 154.

He said to them, "Why are you so afraid? Have you still no
faith?" (v. 40)

At this point, the disciples are likely shocked and awed. They
are shocked *by* their awe. The dozing master has hushed the storm.
Do you hear the eerie quiet? Picture the previously roiling waters
now like a plane of glass. Not a wave can be seen across the flat
surface of the deep, save the soft ripple from the boat itself. The
wind has stopped. The clouds have cleared. The scene ought to be
cheerful, but it is actually quite spooky.

"F-f-faith?" one of the stunned men might stammer. "Faith in
what?"

Well, first of all, that storms serve a purpose. Do you think
Jesus just likes to watch his creatures squirm? No, we aren't just
floating around in the chaos of life, victims of happenstance and
fortune. We do not have the god of the deists, but the God of
Abraham and Isaac. We are subject to the God who set the galax-
ies in motion, spun the planets on their axes, poured the ancient
seas, summons thunder with his fists, makes the mountains his
footstool, commands the fires and the rains. We serve the God
who is everlasting and all-seeing, a strong fortress and a mighty
warrior. We worship this God who tabernacles with his people,
who ultimately has done so by inhabiting flesh. This God will
never leave us hanging—not even on a cross—because his death
becomes our death (Rom. 6:8; 2 Tim. 2:11) and he did not stay
dead.

So the bad things that happen to us not only are not outside
of his sovereignty, they are not outside of his plan. We may not
know what God is doing in our suffering, but we can trust that he
is doing something!

Second, we can have faith, oddly enough, that no one dies
early. He knows the number of hairs on our heads (Luke 12:7) and
the number of our days. It has been appointed to man once to die
(Heb. 9:27), and no one can take from you what God has allotted
to you. So if you're going to die on a boat on the ocean, you are

going to die on a boat on the ocean. But if you're not, then you're not. This should not be cause for worry but cause for confidence, because the promise for the Christian is that dying is to enter the heavenly life where there is no death. So Paul's modus operandi was, for instance, "to live is Christ, and to die is gain" (Phil. 1:21).

I was discussing our mission trips to Honduras with some church folks once, and the subject came up that San Pedro Sula, the city we travel through on our annual journey to the country, had recently been named the most violent city in the world. The shadow of fear quickly entered the conversation. I jokingly reminded our friends: "If Jesus wants you to die in Honduras, your not going to Honduras won't matter one bit. You will go to bed one night and wake up in the morning dead in Honduras!"

Still the cry goes up, "We are perishing!"

Well, of course we are. But not a day sooner than God has ordained. And all will be well.

Third, when we put together faith that trials have a purpose and faith that no one dies early, they basically amount to faith in God. Real, genuine, self-forgetful, self-abandoned faith in God. The kind of faith that says, "Though he slay me, I will hope in him" (Job 13:15). The kind of faith that believes our God will deliver us from the fiery furnace, but even if he doesn't, we will still keep from idolatry (Dan. 3:17–18). The kind of faith that says, "We do not know what to do, but our eyes are on you" (2 Chron. 20:12).

> And they were filled with great fear and said to one another, "Who then is this, that even the wind and the sea obey him?" (Mark 4:41)

This slack-jawed question reminds me of Isaiah 63:1:

> Who is this who comes from Edom, in crimsoned garments from Bozrah, he who is splendid in his apparel, marching in the greatness of his strength? "It is I, speaking in righteousness, mighty to save."

## The Dangerous Glory

Something strikes me about the disciples' response. Jesus has already calmed the storm. And Mark 4:41 says "they were filled with great fear" *after* the storm is calmed. Why?

You would think that after Jesus has been stirred to consciousness and obligingly sends the trouble packing, the disciples would be hooting and hollering with joy, slapping each other's backs, and giving each other high fives. Instead, they go from frantic to frozen. We must ask why.

I think the answer is this: they are mortified at this moment because of the sheer awesomeness of his authoritative power on overwhelming display, but also because, from the backs of their minds comes the deeply unsettling realization that if Jesus controls the storms, it means that when there's a storm, he not only didn't stop it but allowed it, *ordained* it, even.

Don't we see this wrestling every time a tragedy strikes? Some cataclysmic natural disaster lays waste to cities and people, and the world demands that religious people answer for their God. And Christians get embarrassed. We want to be God's defense attorneys. We want to explain God's sovereignty away. We want to say: "Well, he's in control, but not of stuff like that. He's in control, but not of the bad stuff. That stuff just sort of, you know, happens."

Biblically speaking, this is nonsense.

There are a lot of reasons for difficulties and sufferings in the world, but a powerless, passive God *isn't one of them*.

This is why I hate the prosperity gospel so much. I hate it, hate it, hate it. I smell sulfur when I hear it, get a bitter taste in my mouth. The prosperity gospelists promise things God never promised and deny things he has ordained from of old, and in the end these heretics deflect sovereignty away from the triune God and toward the out-of-tune believer, and thereby send people to hell. And any theology that, when believed, sends people to hell is to be abominated.

People often ask why I occasionally angrily criticize prosperity preachers such as Joel Osteen. This is why: because he's sending people to hell. He gives people who are suffering, poor, and in need of a theology of the cross of Christ a nonexistent genie in a magic lamp, and when they aren't fixed, healed, or made prosperous, great doubt and confusion inevitably set in. They think: "Maybe God isn't loving. Maybe God isn't powerful. Maybe I don't have real faith." All because the prosperity gospelist has invited naïve people to ask comfort into their hearts and invite material goods to be their personal lord and savior. All their faith has been placed in mortal things and not on the God who purposes pain.

But the God of the Scriptures, the one true God, is sovereign over all things. And that is scary sometimes. It is spiritually discombobulating.

"Who then is this?" the disciples wonder. This is the question all of us must answer. It is a variation of the follow-up question Jesus poses in Mark 8:29 to see if they've learned anything: "Who do you say that I am?"

He is God. He is the God who ordained the storm of the cross, who did not spare his only Son, the man of sorrows, the suffering servant, who bore our afflictions in order to redeem us from sin and eternal suffering. And because he ordained the cross to be our redemption, he ordained our suffering to make us more like Jesus.

This is the whole point of Christianity! It is to glorify Jesus. It is that the Lamb might receive the reward of his suffering!

This God, incarnate in Jesus Christ, our Savior and Lord, is the God who rules and loves. We serve a far better God than all the false gods, and not just because he's real. All the gods of the world promise health, wealth, and satisfaction, and *then don't even deliver it.* Our God may take us through a fire, but we will come out refined. He may take us through a storm, but we will come out washed. He may ask us to take up our crosses in this life, but he will deliver us safe and sound for all eternity.

The miracles that demonstrate Jesus's control of the natural world—his command of food and wine, of fish and fig trees, of waters and winds—reveal Christ as sovereign Lord, as master of the universe, as maker and therefore commander of the laws of nature. The glory these miracles reveal is that of the Creator God come to bend creation back to order. Today, the Spirit of God is roaming the earth, seeking whom he may revive, opening eyes and hearts to behold the glory of the risen Son, who commands the earth from his place seated next to his Father. He is making all things new, and he's doing it from his throne.

In my book *Gospel Wakefulness*, I included an important chapter on depression, and in that chapter I included this anecdote:

> There is a story often attributed to Robert Louis Stevenson of a ship caught in a dreadful storm off a rocky coast. The hurricane winds, driving rain, and heaving waves threatened to drive the ship and its passengers into destruction. In the midst of the terror, one daring man pulled himself up the slippery stairs of the ship's hold to the deck, fearful of what he'd see. The ship tossed steeply; creaking and cracking pierced the steady whoosh of the angry sea. The moonlight in the heavy rain did not allow much vision, but the sailor held fast and gazed across the deck to the wheel of the ship. There he saw the pilot at his post gripping the wheel strongly, and bit by bit steering the ship out to sea. The pilot spotted the terrified spy and gave him a smile. Impressed, the passenger returned to the hold and sounded the news: "I have seen the face of the pilot, and he smiled at me. All is well."[4]

Imagine with me if you will, however, knowing what we know about our sovereign Lord from Mark 4, this alternative ending:

> The curious passenger made his way back down to the hold, slipping on the wet steps, rocked side to side violently against

[4] Jared C. Wilson, *Gospel Wakefulness* (Wheaton, IL: Crossway, 2011), 161–62.

the walls, hand sliding down the rail. He stood unsteadily before his comrades and sounded the news over the roar of the storm outside: "I have made my way to see the pilot. He is asleep in the stern. All is well."

Jesus doesn't just walk around like he made the place. He rests like he does, too.

# 5

# He Has Done All Things Well

"In the beginning, God created the heavens and the earth" (Gen. 1:1). God spoke light into existence. He separated the land from the water. He created every growing thing. He created the sun, the moon, and the stars. He ordered the seas to teem with fish. He filled the skies with birds. He placed an endless variety of crawling animals on the earth. And at the end of each day in creation, he stepped back to survey his work and declared, "This is good."

Then he made a man. Out of the dust of the ground, God made man, breathing life into the mud from his very self. And he made a helper for the man, taking one of his ribs and fashioning from it a woman.

After completing man and woman, the crown of all his creation—conscious, relational, spiritual, creative beings made in God's very image—God stepped back to survey the entire scene (Gen. 1:31) and said, "Oh, this is all very good."

That is how God made us and what God declared us. Unspoiled and unfallen, Adam and Eve were given dominion under God's authority over the garden, charged with tending and cultivating it, and with producing offspring upon offspring to fill the civilization they were commissioned to grow.

What God had done, he had done with all the divine excellence of his holy power.

What Adam and Eve did, they did with all the perilous potential of their free will.

God placed a tree in the garden, forbidding Adam and Eve to eat from it. The tree stood as a living reminder that God was God and they were not. And ever since Adam and Eve filled their bellies with disobedience, sin has been eating us all from the inside out.

The fall had far-reaching and eternally devastating ramifications. In Romans 8:22, Paul says the world that God created good is now groaning for redemption. And we are, too (v. 23). The rebellion was cosmic, and therefore so is the corruption. When we read of God's curse of the ground (Gen. 3:17), we are to understand that it extends far beyond the literal land and applies to the entire created world, including our bodies. We get tired now, we get hurt now, we get sick now, we die now. It is our very flesh and bone that suffer from this cancerous anti-creation.

It's quite possible that the condition called leprosy is the most vivid illustration of the corruption of the human body since the fall. Certainly the culture of Jesus's day thought so. Lepers were considered not simply medically infectious but religiously unclean. You could catch not just flesh-eating bacteria from them but unholiness. The Jews had plenty of Scripture to support this position. Leviticus 13–14 is a lengthy example. So they weren't exactly making this stuff up. It came from God.

But then God himself came. And while he inhabited the same flesh susceptible to leprosy (contra Athanasius[1]), he dared to touch the lepers as if he didn't. And he touched them not simply with compassion—but, oh, what compassion!—but with the express purpose of restoring with love what had become degraded by sin.

Jesus's posture toward the laws about leprosy helps us see the purpose in all the miraculous healings discussed over the next two chapters. The way he went out of his way to touch the untouch-

---

[1] Athanasius, *On the Incarnation*, 4.21, trans. Archibald Robertson (London: D. Nutt, 1885), 32–34.

able, to miraculously clean the unclean, speaks to the connection between Jesus's healings and the forgiveness of sins. Michael Williams elaborates:

> The healing miracles were not separate or merely a benevolent addenda to his proclamation. . . . They were themselves embodied proclamations of the nature of the kingdom.[2]

Diseases and disabilities remind us of the curse and the law. But the kingdom brings the antidote: the forgiveness of sins in the fulfillment of the law.

This vital connection between the kingdom and the law is why Jesus keeps stubbornly healing on the Sabbath.

## Defining the Relationship

Once, Jesus and his disciples are walking through a field on the Sabbath, and the hungry disciples begin plucking off the heads of grain to eat (Matt. 12:1–8). The Pharisees immediately confront them about violating the Sabbath regulations against work. Jesus responds by citing a few historical examples of such "profaning," but then says something quite startling, at least to the religious leaders:

> I tell you, something greater than the temple is here. And if you had known what this means, "I desire mercy, and not sacrifice," you would not have condemned the guiltless. For the Son of Man is lord of the Sabbath. (Matt. 12:6–8)

"Something greater than the temple is here." These are the words of a revolutionary. This is a shot across the bow. This is ideological treason—except that Jesus is setting himself up not as the enemy of the temple and its laws but as their Maker.

One of my favorite scenes from the Gospels occurs during the

---

[2] Michael D. Williams, *Far as the Curse Is Found: The Covenant Story of Redemption* (Phillipsburg, NJ: Presbyterian and Reformed, 2005), 284.

cleansing of the temple in the later part of Jesus's ministry. In a sort of "blink and you might miss it" moment, in Mark 11:16 we see Jesus standing in the temple court, preventing people from passing through it on their way to everyday business. They are treating the temple complex like a shortcut, and Jesus, after driving out the moneychangers and buyers, puts himself in the middle of the thoroughfare and starts directing traffic! I can just hear Jesus's very Gandalfian "You shall not pass!"

That image reminds us, however, that the Jewish religion, established by God as the outworking of his gracious election and deliverance of the Jewish people, had come to be thought of as the means of deliverance itself. And once you begin "using" something, you begin abusing it, taking it for granted, and turning it into a cheap idol.

Now Jesus has come claiming to be the lord of the Sabbath, and further, to highlight the intrinsic love of God and the dawning kingdom's operating system of grace, he says, "The Sabbath was made for man, not man for the Sabbath" (Mark 2:27).

To illustrate this radical redefinition, Jesus not only allows his disciples to pluck grain on the Sabbath; he insists on healing people on the Sabbath. A man with dropsy, healed in the very house of a religious leader, is but one example:

> One Sabbath, when he went to dine at the house of a ruler of the Pharisees, they were watching him carefully. And behold, there was a man before him who had dropsy. And Jesus responded to the lawyers and Pharisees, saying, "Is it lawful to heal on the Sabbath, or not?" But they remained silent. Then he took him and healed him and sent him away. And he said to them, "Which of you, having a son or an ox that has fallen into a well on a Sabbath day, will not immediately pull him out?" And they could not reply to these things. (Luke 14:1–6)

First, the logic is impeccable. No one is more logical than Jesus, in fact. He makes the parallel quite plain: if you had a son—or even

an ox—in trouble on the Sabbath, you would not hesitate to commence a rescue. Who could dispute that? Only the most callous
of men, and none of the Pharisees is at this moment willing to out
himself as one of them.

Second, once again, healing on the Sabbath shows both Jesus's
authority over the law *and* the finality of the law. In fact, embracing the gospel of the kingdom of God and its gospel entailments
means to cease from your striving, to rest from your works as God
has rested from his, to act as if the work of new creation is accom-
plished. Hebrews 4:1–11 elaborates:

> Therefore, while the promise of entering his rest still stands,
> let us fear lest any of you should seem to have failed to reach
> it. For good news came to us just as to them, but the message
> they heard did not benefit them, because they were not united
> by faith with those who listened. For we who have believed
> enter that rest, as he has said,
>
>> "As I swore in my wrath,
>> 'They shall not enter my rest,'"
>
> although his works were finished from the foundation of the
> world. For he has somewhere spoken of the seventh day in
> this way: "And God rested on the seventh day from all his
> works." And again in this passage he said,
>
>> "They shall not enter my rest."
>
> Since therefore it remains for some to enter it, and those who
> formerly received the good news failed to enter because of
> disobedience, again he appoints a certain day, "Today," say-
> ing through David so long afterward, in the words already
> quoted,
>
>> "Today, if you hear his voice,
>> do not harden your hearts."

For if Joshua had given them rest, God would not have spoken of another day later on. So then, there remains a Sabbath rest for the people of God, for whoever has entered God's rest has also rested from his works as God did from his. Let us therefore strive to enter that rest.

The work of resting from working for salvation proves too hard for many, including most of the Pharisees Jesus encounters, but clearly the relationship between man and Sabbath has been redefined from one of obligation to opportunity, from debit to credit. Thus, Jesus heals on the Sabbath because the kingdom is gospel, not law.

And if we have the eyes to see the other world sparkling in the glory of Jesus's miracles, we will notice the heavenly radiance of that eternal Sabbath rapidly coming, the endless day when creation will be restored to "very good" once again, made *better* than good even, totally absent disease and disability of any kind.

In redefining the relationship between man and the Sabbath (and therefore the law) through the kingdom, Jesus redefines the relationship between man and God himself. Notice Jesus compares the man with dropsy in Luke 14 to something very dear to his audience—a valuable ox or a precious son. In persisting in his mission to reach the untouchables, Jesus is affirming the "image of God" inherent to each one of them. Where religious Jews see an unclean man, Jesus sees a son.

This redefining of the relationship—calling sinners "children"—carries through to our next reflection.

## The Healing within the Healing

The depths of God's love in the gospel of his Son, Jesus Christ, are fathoms enough for the baptizing of the universe and at the same time safe enough for a baby to play in. The same ocean that offers the foot-soaking shore offers core-slicing trenches veiled in mystery, depths we may never see. I think we see this glorious truth in the miracle of the raising of Jairus's daughter, interrupted by the healing of the woman with the bloody discharge. Here is a refresher from Mark's account:

> And when Jesus had crossed again in the boat to the other side, a great crowd gathered about him, and he was beside the sea. Then came one of the rulers of the synagogue, Jairus by name, and seeing him, he fell at his feet and implored him earnestly, saying, "My little daughter is at the point of death. Come and lay your hands on her, so that she may be made well and live." And he went with him.
>
> And a great crowd followed him and thronged about him. And there was a woman who had had a discharge of blood for twelve years, and who had suffered much under many physicians, and had spent all that she had, and was no better but rather grew worse. She had heard the reports about Jesus and came up behind him in the crowd and touched his garment. For she said, "If I touch even his garments, I will be made well." And immediately the flow of blood dried up, and she felt in her body that she was healed of her disease. And Jesus, perceiving in himself that power had gone out from him, immediately turned about in the crowd and said, "Who touched my garments?" And his disciples said to him, "You see the crowd pressing around you, and yet you say, 'Who touched me?'" And he looked around to see who had done it. But the woman, knowing what had happened to her, came in fear and trembling and fell down before him and told him the whole truth. And he said to her, "Daughter, your faith has made you well; go in peace, and be healed of your disease."
>
> While he was still speaking, there came from the ruler's house some who said, "Your daughter is dead. Why trouble the Teacher any further?" But overhearing what they said, Jesus said to the ruler of the synagogue, "Do not fear, only believe." And he allowed no one to follow him except Peter and James and John the brother of James. They came to the house of the ruler of the synagogue, and Jesus saw a commotion, people weeping and wailing loudly. And when he had

entered, he said to them, "Why are you making a commotion and weeping? The child is not dead but sleeping." And they laughed at him. But he put them all outside and took the child's father and mother and those who were with him and went in where the child was. Taking her by the hand he said to her, "Talitha cumi," which means, "Little girl, I say to you, arise." And immediately the girl got up and began walking (for she was twelve years of age), and they were immediately overcome with amazement. And he strictly charged them that no one should know this, and told them to give her something to eat. (Mark 5:21–43)

We will return to a fuller treatment of the raising of Jairus's daughter in chapter 9, but for now I offer three gospel applications of this passage as a whole that may help us see the way the kingdom redefines boundaries and social structures, and thus help us see the depths of Christ's love.

*First, we can say that quite evidently there are no little people in the kingdom of God!* Jairus is a ruler of the synagogue, a high muckety muck, if you will. The woman clearly is not. In fact, she is considered continually unclean, and therefore untouchable, because of her condition (Lev. 15:25), which most certainly informs the way she seeks out her healing. She tries to steal it, in effect. And yet, Jesus makes time for her. He could turn around in a huff, treating her as an irritant or an annoyance. But he doesn't.

Over and over we see what kinds of people Jesus goes out of his way to fraternize with, consistently setting the first last and the last first (Matt. 19:30). When the disciples are trying to cordon the children off, hustling them off to "children's church" perhaps, it is the grown-ups he rebukes (vv. 13–14). It's the sick who need a doctor (9:12) and the poor in spirit who receive the blessing (5:3), so when you tug on Jesus's garment, he doesn't sigh or roll his eyes. He loves to be pestered. Pester him. His love is that deep.

*Second, we see in this passage that a weak faith and a strong faith receive the same measure of grace.* Jairus comes—as far as we can tell—fully convinced. He knows that Jesus *can* heal his daughter and he trusts that Jesus *will*, so he approaches Jesus directly. The woman tries stealth. She trusts that Jesus *can* heal her, but she isn't trusting that he *will*. She's been burned too many times in the past. She's not willing to risk being rejected due to her condition or because of Jesus's apparent hurry. And when finally confronted, she is full of fear and trembling.

But what does he call the woman? "Daughter" (Mark 5:34). He is equating her essentially with Jairus's daughter, and more importantly, establishing her relationship to himself and the Father. This is more wonderful evidence that it is not a strong faith that saves but a true faith. It is proof that the most beat-up and beat-down mustard seed-size faith, tattered and tiny, receives the eternal fullness of the glorious riches of Christ. It need not be big; it need only be real. That's how deep God's love is.

*Finally, the way this encounter develops shows us the bigger picture, that on the way to resurrection, our salvation is part of the story.* On his way to raise Jairus's daughter from the dead, Jesus heals the woman and makes her part of the story of the raising of Jairus's daughter. She becomes an integral part, in fact, because it is while Jesus delays his journey to care for the woman that the little girl passes from severe illness into death. And Jesus's plan for Jairus's daughter is to raise her, not simply heal her.

The narrative here is a micro-picture of the bigger story: Jesus is on his way to die and rise again. Along the way, he is teaching, healing, exorcising demons, eating, sleeping, welcoming, and worshiping. He has a plan, and he will get there at the right time. He is on the Father's business, determined to give himself up that he may be lifted up, but in the meantime, there is *time*. And all who desire his touch get it. (I find it special, too, that Mark, who is the most eager of the Gospel writers to get to the cross and therefore produces the shortest and most urgent-toned of the Synoptic Gospels, has the longest version of this account of the three. It is as if he wants to slow down to reflect Jesus's slowing down.)

Like the Bible that reveals it, the gospel is not about us but *for* us. The story is chiefly about God's glory. But in the gospel, we are partakers of that glory. So part of the story of Christ's death and resurrection is the story of the captives being freed from sin and shame. I am grateful he made time for me! Before the world began, he was making space for me! And in heaven now, Jesus is preparing space for me!

Paul writes in Romans 8:32, "He who did not spare his own Son but gave him up for us all, how will he not also with him graciously give us all things?" So as we rush headlong toward the second coming of Christ, there is time enough for the salvation of all who trust in him. He will not come until all God's children are accounted for in salvation. He is not really slow; he is patient, and there's a difference. Peter says in 2 Peter 3:9: "The Lord is not slow to fulfill his promise as some count slowness, but is patient toward you, not wishing that any should perish, but that all should reach repentance."

The gospel story is about Christ's exaltation, but our healing is an integral part of the story—indeed, it is part of his exaltation. The love of Christ is so deep, there is more than enough for you if you want it.

## Waiting on the World to Change

I find the story of the healing of the paralytic at the pool of Bethesda heartbreaking and exhilarating at the same time:

> Now there is in Jerusalem by the Sheep Gate a pool, in Aramaic called Bethesda, which has five roofed colonnades. In these lay a multitude of invalids—blind, lame, and paralyzed. One man was there who had been an invalid for thirty-eight years. When Jesus saw him lying there and knew that he had already been there a long time, he said to him, "Do you want to be healed?" The sick man answered him, "Sir, I have no one to put me into the pool when the water is stirred up, and while I am going another steps down before me." Jesus said to him,

"Get up, take up your bed, and walk." And at once the man
was healed, and he took up his bed and walked. Now that day
was the Sabbath. (John 5:2–9)

I try to put myself in the place of this man who has been paralyzed for nearly four decades, who has come within feet of his pro-
spective healing probably on multiple occasions. I'm not sure I can
wrap my mind around the helplessness and despair he deals with
on a daily basis. I can see people stepping over him to get their healing, kicking him in the process, stepping *on* him probably. And yet
I do know what it is like to have no hope but God. And I do know
what it is like to finally receive healing from my despair, which was
the first affliction the Lord released me from before restoring other
blessings I had long given up on.

Sometimes we miss the blessing because we are looking for it
anywhere but in Jesus. And, of course, as this man's story indicates,
some in this world are seeking healing who do not even know there
is a Jesus to seek it from. But our Shepherd is good, and he is outside the pen looking for the lost.

The Bethesda paralytic has waited a long time for healing that
has always seemed within reach. This is a good metaphor for the
nation of Israel. Bound up in the culture of Jesus's day are thousands of years of bondage, anxiety, hope, expectation—a terrible
and spiritual angst. In the meantime, many are jockeying for position, promoting their man or their way as the fulfillment of all the
hopes for deliverance. There are so many religious sects, would-be
messiahs, and revolutionary splinter cells, so many pastors and po-
liticos. Israel will get its consolation, but how? No one can pardon
her sins, and every time she gets her hopes up, they are dashed by
yet another devastating setback.

But Jesus comes comforting Israel, speaking tenderly to her,
crying to her that her striving is finished, that her warfare is over,
that her sins are forgiven, that she will receive a blessing of joy so
big that the thousands of years of hardship will seem but a blip on
the radar of eternity. The kingdom of God is at hand. If you want

healing, he says, it is yours for the taking. Jesus tells Israel to take up her bed and walk.

So many in Jesus's day are waiting for the world to change, but their vision for the world is much too small. The stepped-on assume that the coming of the kingdom means simply the ousting of the exploiters. The powers that be assume it means a final dismissal of the untouchables. But the ground is level at the foot of the cross. There is no partiality, and the kingdom is an equal-opportunity offender and healer. So Jesus extends his hands of healing to help the lowly, such as the man with the withered hand (Matt. 12:9–13); the powerful, such as the centurion (8:5–13); the friends of his friends, such as Peter's mother-in-law (vv. 14–15); and the enemies of his enemies, such as the thief on the cross (Luke 23:39–43).

"This was to fulfill what was spoken by the prophet Isaiah: 'He took our illnesses and bore our diseases'" (Matt. 8:17).

## Putting Everything Just So

Albert Wolters says that Jesus's miracles constituted "a reinstatement of creaturely living as intended by God."[3] The disarray of fallen creation is the result of human rebellion against God's design. We creatures said: "No, not that way. This way." But God will not let us have the last word. He comes graciously, putting things back into order. This good news is big news, because it means that God is not content to merely forgive our sins—as huge as that is!—but actually counteracts the effects and consequences of our sins as well. This is why Jesus keeps connecting his miraculous healings to the forgiveness of sins. "He comes to make his blessings flow far as the curse is found."[4]

The healing of the paralytic in Capernaum is just one example:

And when he returned to Capernaum after some days, it was reported that he was at home. And many were gathered to-

---

[3] Albert Wolters, quoted in Randy Alcorn, *Heaven* (Carol Stream, IL: Tyndale House, 2004), 89.
[4] Isaac Watts, "Joy to the World" (1719).

gether, so that there was no more room, not even at the door.
And he was preaching the word to them. (Mark 2:1–2)

We should stop at this point to be reminded that the point
of Jesus's ministry is not his wonders but his word. Mark 1:38
reminds us that preaching is why he "came out." Many have gathered, crammed fully into the room, shoulder to shoulder. And Jesus
is preaching, which is the most important aspect of his ministry.
This may seem like an arbitrary point, but it is important to keep
in mind, given what ensues:

> And they came, bringing to him a paralytic carried by four
> men. And when they could not get near him because of the
> crowd, they removed the roof above him, and when they had
> made an opening, they let down the bed on which the para-
> lytic lay. (Mark 2:3–4)

The roof on this house is composed of only a few layers of
branches and caked mud. It is not hard to "unroof." Nevertheless,
what loving friends! That they will vandalize personal property to
get their friend before the Lord's face shows a remarkable amount
of compassion for him and trust in the Lord.

Now, they get this poor guy right before Jesus's face, and their
friend is in the most helpless state possible. He is presented totally
vulnerable to the worker of wonders, and Jesus says something
startling: "Son, your sins are forgiven" (v. 5).

Notice first that Jesus refers to the man as "son." And if this
declaration of relationship—declaring an outsider a member of
the family—isn't scandalous enough, Jesus declares the man's sins
forgiven.

The religious leaders naturally freak out over this pronouncement. Jesus is doing something much more provocative than
physically healing the man. In their estimation, he is committing
blasphemy. Why? Because only God can forgive sins.

Jesus's pronouncement is scandalous in our day for a completely different reason. "Your sins are forgiven" is offensive today because we don't think of sin as the fundamental problem of human existence. The Jews of Jesus's day did. But the expectations and motivations today are very similar to those of Jesus's day, theological presuppositions notwithstanding. Even preachers identifying themselves as Christian today downplay the existence of sin and the primacy of the cross in order to present the faith as predominantly a self-improvement program. Like many who clamored about Jesus, many churches today are filled with people eager to trade the gospel for a miracle rather than embracing the miracle *of* the gospel.

Even in religious clothing, this is worldliness. To deny one's intrinsic spiritual debt to God and seek gifts apart from being restored to the Giver is the way of fallen creation. And getting right to the heart of the matter of new creation, Jesus's words remind us that there are worse things than being paralyzed for the rest of your life.

"Your sins are forgiven." Forgiveness is great, but what it assumes is not very seeker sensitive.

Is Jesus saying that the man's paralysis is the result of his personal sin? I don't think so. Jesus himself speaks against such notions elsewhere (John 9:1–3; Luke 13:4–5).

I think, instead, it's the same reason that Jesus won't be distracted by diversionary chit-chat with the Samaritan woman at the well (John 4). I think it's the same reason why Jesus refuses to condemn the woman caught in adultery but still sends her away with some choice words (John 8:11). I think it's connected to the way this miracle-working Jesus keeps saying the reason he came was to preach (Mark 1:38; 2:2; Matt. 12:39), not perform miracles. It is because we can always count on Jesus to shoot straight. He will always be honest with us about what we most need.

If Jesus is putting everything in its place, he must start with the fundamental creation order. He must put us in our place. The cross looms over his ministry, casting a shadow that looks an awful lot like that tree in the garden, the one that says, "God is God, and you are not." Jesus's forgiveness of sins communicates this same message.

Think of how many times in prayer or study we bring problems or issues to the Lord—and they are usually things he's certainly willing to deal with and address—but they amount to subterfuges, conscious or unconscious, from the real matters of our hearts. We often present things for Jesus to heal *other* than what he really means to get at in us. We love for Jesus to fix our circumstances and our pains, but we often don't want him doing the invasive surgery his gospel is designed for. So we pile up the fig leaves. What Jesus first says to the paralyzed man is a startling reminder that there are far better things than being healthy all your life.

Jesus gave the man the greatest gift he could receive: eternal pardon. The rest was gravy. Suppose Jesus had only healed the man's body but not his soul? He might have danced until his dying day and then suffered for all eternity. On the other hand, suppose Jesus had not subsequently ladled that circumstantial miracle upon the eternal one. What would have happened? The man would have lived out his days still paralyzed, only to die and emerge in the resurrection to come with dancing legs he could never imagine.

When Jesus heals us physically and blesses us circumstantially, he is providing signposts to the scope of his atoning work, to the resurrection to come and the infinite bliss of the Lamb-lit new heaven and earth. He wants us to terminate not on the signs but on the Signified. And this is also why he often denies us these circumstantial blessings. It is likely that not everyone who wanted physical healing from Jesus during his earthly ministry got it. But it is certain that anyone who trusted in him was saved eternally.

The lessons Jesus teaches are hard, as they often involve great suffering, but they are for our joy, as they involve eternal life.

This is what the gospel of the kingdom announces: the kingdom unshakeable, immortal, immovable, unconquerable. The invincible Christ is King, and he is taking over the neighborhood. But if your heart is set on your own kingdom, you will find yourself set outside of the courts, into the outer darkness that manifests your inner darkness, when everything gets put in its place.

The religious leaders will not go quietly.

> And immediately Jesus, perceiving in his spirit that they thus questioned within themselves, said to them, "Why do you question these things in your hearts? Which is easier, to say to the paralytic, 'Your sins are forgiven,' or to say, 'Rise, take up your bed and walk'?" (Mark 2:8–9)

Oh, now here is a sticky wicket. One would think it is easier to say, "Your sins are forgiven," because miracles of physical healing require much more visible power and we can't see inside a heart. But the reality is that it is harder to say, "Your sins are forgiven," because that is something only God can do. Miracles are certainly rare throughout history, even in biblical times, but there are still scriptural examples of them being performed by many with apparent access to supernatural power. Pharaoh's sorcerers could work up some satanic wonders. I think this is what Jesus is getting at.

In any event, Jesus goes ahead and covers all the bases by healing the man. He once again graciously condescends to grumblers, adding another grace to the infinite grace he's already given the paralyzed man. Thus, he shows what miracles are truly meant to show: the glory of Jesus as forgiver:

> "But that you may know that the Son of Man has authority on earth to forgive sins"—he said to the paralytic—"I say to you, rise, pick up your bed, and go home." And he rose and immediately picked up his bed and went out before them all, so that they were all amazed and glorified God, saying, "We never saw anything like this!" (vv. 10–12)

I imagine the crowd parting like the Red Sea while the symbol of God's faithfulness passes through, dancing.

Can we go back to the first verse, though? Mark 2:1 tells us that "he was at home." Many take this reference to mean that the setting is Jesus's own home. It could very well be Levi's home, and many argue that way, too. After all, didn't Jesus say the Son of Man had no place to lay his head (Matt. 8:20)?

There are a variety of perspectives with varying strengths and weaknesses. I don't know that we may infer from Matthew 8:20 that Jesus is what we today would call "homeless" any more than we may infer from Mark 2:1 that Jesus owns a house. But it seems likely that the place is somewhere Jesus feels at home.

In any event, imagine for a moment that this is Jesus's house, or at least a house he feels at home in. Can you imagine tearing a hole in Jesus's roof so as to barge in and interrupt him, and then expect him to do something other than deliver a rebuke or turn you over to the authorities? I mean, *the nerve*.

Perhaps this is one of the sins Jesus is forgiving.

The home of God on earth was traditionally thought to be the temple, and there was no way you could enter it so presumptuously and expect to live, let alone be received with welcome. But something greater than the temple is here. The furniture is getting rearranged. Jesus is putting everything back in place, setting things to rights, getting everything just so.

The gates have been thrown open, the doors raised. The hope of glory has come down from heaven. He has left his own home to come to ours, and in his atoning work, he rips the roof off the temple, tearing the veil of the Most Holy Place, that we may be ushered into the glory of God and be "at home" with him.

## He Has Done All Things "Good"

After Jesus heals the paralytic at home, "they were all amazed and glorified God, saying, 'We never saw anything like this!'" (Mark 2:12). The Lord is working his new creation, and he wants us to stand alongside him at each stage and see that it is good.

There is a similar response after his healing of the deaf-mute in the Decapolis. We find this story in Mark 7, beginning like this: "And they brought to him a man who was deaf and had a speech impediment, and they begged him to lay his hand on him" (v. 32).

We might assume that the "they" in this verse refers to a group of friends, like those who lowered the paralytic through the roof. It is a great love to bring people to Jesus, trusting that he can do what he says he can. One of the chief ways we can do this today is by interceding for others, bringing them to Jesus in prayer and asking him to have mercy on them.

In this instance, Jesus takes the subject away from the crowd (v. 33). Why? Perhaps to enhance the personal connection with the man. Perhaps because we each have to do our own business with the Lord, not anyone else's. But perhaps also because Jesus is continuing to refuse to be anyone's magician. He is not an entertainer. His miracles are not meant to elicit oohs and aahs but to elicit: "Ah, Lord GOD! It is you who have made the heavens and the earth by your great power and by your outstretched arm! Nothing is too hard for you" (Jer. 32:17). This seems evident from his further instructions in Mark 7:36.

Jesus heals the man in a most interesting way: "[H]e put his fingers into his ears and after spitting touched his tongue" (v. 33). Why?

This is difficult. There are no obvious references for what Jesus does here in terms of equating it with any kind of parallel ritual known from the time. The closest biblical parallels we have are Jesus's healing of the blind men in John 9 and Mark 8, which we will discuss in our next chapter. In the former instance, Jesus makes mud out of dirt and spit, and applies it to the man's eyes, and in the latter, Jesus simply spits directly on the man's eyes.

Maybe Jesus puts his fingers in the man's ears for a very mundane reason, simply to indicate what he's going to do (cure his deafness). Perhaps the man cannot read lips. The use of his spit is something different altogether.

I wonder whether, by touching his own saliva, Jesus is providing a symbolic proclamation of his incarnation. Jesus the sinless man is the image of what we are supposed to be. And just as the miracles show us the world as God intends for it to be—unbroken—Jesus is connecting his perfect tongue with the way this man's tongue is meant to be. Deafness, blindness, muteness—all such disabilities are signs that we live in a broken world. These things will not exist in the new heaven and the new earth.

So when Jesus heals someone, we're supposed to fixate on Jesus. He's giving us a window into the day and place when there will be no need for healing because all will be healed. There will be a day and place when those who believe in Jesus will be transformed and glorified into perfect reflections of Jesus. So maybe Jesus is saying with his actions: "Your tongue is supposed to be like my tongue. And when your mouth works right, it's because it is made in the image of mine."

> And looking up to heaven, he sighed and said to him, "Ephphatha," that is, "Be opened." And his ears were opened, his tongue was released, and he spoke plainly. (Mark 7:34–35)

I like to imagine the guy had perfect hearing and could recite Scripture with a voice like James Earl Jones's.

Many of us are waiting on deliverances and healings of various kinds. We continue to pray to God for them, and should they come, we will be so happy. And yet, when we all get to heaven, *what a day of rejoicing that will be*! Our ears will be opened, our tongues released, sickness and death dissolving at the finish line. "Be healed," Jesus will say in that twinkling of an eye, and we will be glorified. I am glad when God heals me of my temporary ailments, but someday I'll be much gladder.

These miracles are windows into heaven, where everything has always been good. That place is rushing powerfully into this place, and we who are caught up in heaven's overflow will be made suitable for the new digs.

Here is the response that reminds me of the response to the healing of the paralytic: "And they were astonished beyond measure, saying, 'He has done all things well. He even makes the deaf hear and the mute speak'" (Mark 7:37).

But oh, kids, that's just the beginning! For when Jesus looks up to say "Ephphatha. . . . Be opened" (v. 34), he's not just talking about the ears and the eyes of the deaf and the blind, but about heaven itself. Heaven, be opened! Heaven, spill out your glory.

And because it was the Father's will, heaven has given forth its King, its honored Son, the firstborn of all creation. Heaven has opened up and given us God in the flesh. In these miracles, heaven has opened up and shown us glimpses of new life beyond the veil, glimpses of life *after* life after death. Heaven has opened up in the life and ministry of Jesus, showing us the kingdom coming to earth, renewing all things. He makes the deaf hear and the mute speak, yes, but behold, he also, according to Revelation 21:5, is making all things new!

And just as he made all things good, he does all things well! So the newness is well done. It glistens with eternity; it has the glow of the radiance of the glory of God about it. When he gives life, he gives it abundantly (John 10:10). When he gives a burden and a yoke, he makes sure it's a light one and an easy one (Matt. 11:30). When he welcomes the weary, he gives them rest (v. 28). When he sets people free, they are free indeed (John 8:36). He does all things well.

He justifies us. He sanctifies us. He glorifies us. His work grounds our adoption, our union, our reconciliation.

*He does all things well.*

Look back over your life. If you see valleys, see how the Lord brought you out of them time and time again. His mercies are new every morning (Lam. 3:22–23). His steadfast love endures forever (Ps. 100:5). His promises are yes and amen (2 Cor. 1:20). He will not leave you or forsake you (Heb. 13:5). Nothing can separate you from the love of God (Rom. 8:39). No one can snatch you out of his hand (John 10:28). Lo, he is with you always, even to the end of the age (Matt. 28:20).

*He has done all things well.*

But don't just see the valleys; see the mountains. He has given you heights of joy, if you care to see them. At his right hand are pleasures forevermore (Ps. 16:11). He fills you with joy inexpressible and full of glory (1 Pet. 1:8). The joy of the Lord is your strength (Neh. 8:10). He has made your feet like the deer's, setting you secure on the heights (Ps. 18:33), and has lifted you up with wings like eagles (Isa. 40:31). Time and time again, he has brought you through, delivered you, and given you victories expected and unexpected.

*He has done all things well.*

And as you view the majestic peaks of his faithfulness throughout your life, beautiful snowy peaks in a breathtaking mountain range glistening in the light of heaven, see the one standing tall above them, the most high, the Mount Everest of God's faithfulness to you—Mount Calvary, where Christ took your sin and its death to the cross, bore your punishment, casting it away into the void, and thereby declared not "It is mostly done" or "It is begun," but "It. Is. Finished."

*He has declared it very good. He has done all things well.*

# 6

# The Way That Seeing
# Is Believing

There is a difference between seeing and *seeing.*

I officiated at my younger brother Jeremy's wedding to his darling bride, Danielle, in 2012, and I got choked up standing there as I watched him get choked up taking in the beatific vision of his bride appearing at the end of the aisle, her father at her side. It immediately took me back to June 29, 1996, when I saw my wife-to-be, Becky, appear in her bridal gown. Our wedding day was the third anniversary of the day we officially began dating, and I'd known her for a couple of years before that, but despite having seen Becky an abundance of times over five years, seeing her again in that beautiful moment, with the opening strains of Felix Mendelssohn's "Wedding March" filling the church sanctuary, was like seeing her for the first time.

You can't recapture that moment, of course, but you can. The dad's advice to his son in Proverbs 5:18–19 seems to assume so. Sometimes I look at my wife all these years later—quite often, actually, and I promise I'm not trying to brag, because it honestly says more about her than about me—and think: "Good Lord, how did this beautiful person get made? And how did she wind up in the closest possible proximity to me?"

Right before I got married, as I talked to my own dad about

marriage, I made a joke, saying, "Well, what if I fall out of love?" My dad quipped right back, "Then you fall right back in." By God's grace and my wifes loveliness, falling out of love with her has not been easy, but being intoxicated with her love has. But it was still good advice.

There is an echo here and also a foretaste. I recently surveyed a collection of powerful photos of grooms seeing their brides for the first time on their wedding days. As I recall those photos, as I think of my own wedding day and the wedding days of my brother and others, and as I ponder the desire and the imperative to be intoxicated for all time (for better or worse, in richness and in poorness, in sickness and in health, till death do us part), I see an echo of Adam laying eyes on Eve for the first time:

> This at last is bone of my bones
> 　and flesh of my flesh;
> she shall be called Woman,
> 　because she was taken out of Man. (Gen. 2:23)

The first song ever sung (by man, anyway) is *a love song*. Adam is smitten by the vision of his bride for the first time, and music erupts from his mouth.

And there is a foretaste in this moment, and in every moment when a groom spots his bride in her virginal white, as the bridal march whips up, all the stops out, of Christ the bridegroom presenting us, his bride, to himself at the end of days. Dazzling in the reflection of his glory, cloaked in the virgin white of his righteousness given freely to us, the culmination of the lavishing of the riches of his grace draws near. At last. And forever. For Christ and his bride will have that moment of rapturous wedding joy for all eternity. The Lamb will receive the reward of his suffering and of his love—the infinite, worshipful devotion of his spotless bride. "[A]s the bridegroom rejoices over the bride, so shall your God rejoice over you" (Isa. 62:5b).

This marital rapture is encoded in the glory of Jesus manifested in his miracles. But just as a man may look at his wife with eyes wide open and not see her as his bride, we can see Jesus's miracles and not really see them.

The Gospels chronicle four specific instances of Jesus's healing the blind, although it is probable he healed blindness more times than that. What is interesting about these accounts of healings is how inextricable they are from specific doctrinal messages that go much deeper than the mere information that Jesus has the power to cure blindness.

## Depth Perception

The account of the healing of the blind man in Bethsaida appears only in Mark's Gospel, even though the important exchange it sets up between Jesus and Peter is found in all three Synoptics. The way Mark presents the narrative, however, serves to remind us that true information on the real Christ explodes our nice, tidy, self-interested images:

> And they came to Bethsaida. And some people brought to him a blind man and begged him to touch him. And he took the blind man by the hand and led him out of the village, and when he had spit on his eyes and laid his hands on him, he asked him, "Do you see anything?" (Mark 8:22–23)

Jesus spits on the man's eyes. Let that sink in for a minute. Spitting on someone was not then seen as a sign of endearment any more than it is today. When they spit on Jesus (Matt. 27:30), they are not trying to bless him. It's possible, of course, that this is Mark's truncated way of expressing that Jesus touches his own tongue and then applies the saliva to the man's eyes. But this is not how it's expressed, and the stress on "laid his hands on him" implies that Jesus directly spits on the man's eyes.

What is Jesus doing? He may be reminding the man, and by extension us, that one cannot come to truly see until one is willing to identify with the shame and despising of Christ. Or perhaps, as in the other healings of the blind, the move is meant to connect this act of new creation with the act of original creation, when God gave man breath from his own mouth.

> And he looked up and said, "I see people, but they look like trees, walking." (Mark 8:24)

How the man knows what trees look like, we don't know. Maybe he wasn't born blind or maybe he has some sense of what trees are like from having felt them.

> Then Jesus laid his hands on his eyes again; and he opened his eyes, his sight was restored, and he saw everything clearly. (v. 25)

Jesus leaves nothing halfway done. He always finishes the job. There is a spiritual truth here related to our salvation: "[H]e who began a good work in you will bring it to completion at the day of Jesus Christ" (Phil. 1:6).

The two-phase healing of the blind man illustrates the spiritual reality that sometimes we can see but not see. Isaiah's commission was to actually proclaim this message: "Keep on hearing, but do not understand; keep on seeing, but do not perceive" (Isa. 6:9). Jesus even said this was the point of his parables (Matt. 13:13). We see it in the healing of the ten lepers (Luke 17:11–19). All ten are healed physically, but only one responds with glad gratitude in submission to the healer, and Jesus pronounces that fellow forgiven from his sins. All ten get the healing, but only one is able to *get* the healing (if you know what I mean).

It seems, then, that it's quite possible for someone to confess a Jesus he doesn't follow or even for someone to attempt to follow a Jesus she doesn't confess. Both errors betray a failure to truly behold Jesus, for when we do so, we are inevitably changed (2 Cor. 3:18). But we need to have our own faces unveiled first.

The story continues in Mark 8:26: "And he sent him to his

home, saying, 'Do not even enter the village,'" which is an extension of his frequent forbidding of certain people from telling others about his work (as in v. 30).

An exploration of the so-called messianic secret is beyond the scope of this book, but in this context it has an immediate connection to Jesus's desire not to be seen as a magician. He refuses to be anyone's trained miracle monkey. And this command to the man healed from blindness sets up the transition to the well-known passage with Peter's confession. It asks the question, How do you see Jesus?

> And Jesus went on with his disciples to the villages of Caesarea Philippi. And on the way he asked his disciples, "Who do people say that I am?" And they told him, "John the Baptist; and others say, Elijah; and others, one of the prophets." (vv. 27–28)

The cultural perceptions persist today. There are lots of Jesuses running around in the world. We usually worship the one we make in our own image.

> And he asked them, "But who do you say that I am?" (v. 29a)

This is the most crucial question any person can ever face. It may be time for you, in this very moment as you read this book, to come to terms with what you believe about Jesus. Who do you say Jesus is?

Is he a good teacher?

A decent philosopher?

A social revolutionary?

A man sent from God?

It all comes down to this: not "Who does your church say Jesus is?" or "Who does your mama say Jesus is?" or "Who does your daddy say Jesus is?" or "Who do your friends say Jesus is?" but "Who do *you* say Jesus is?"

> Peter answered him, "You are the Christ." (v. 29b)

Jesus is the Christ. The Anointed One. The Messiah. The King. Matthew's Gospel elaborates on the conversation, including Jesus's commendation of Peter's confession and his referencing of Peter's name in establishing the "rock" of the church's saving confession as the foundation of the kingdom (Matt. 16:17–19). One theory has it that Peter directed Mark not to include that part of the exchange once again out of modesty (and you will notice that Mark keeps Jesus's rebuke of Peter in Mark 8:33).

> And he strictly charged them to tell no one about him. (v. 30)

Why? Because they're still dumb. They're still kind of blind. They see, but not fully. "Are those trees walking?" They don't see the full picture yet. They confess him as the Messiah, but they don't quite yet know what Jesus's messiahship entails.

There is a great hinge in Mark's Gospel at this very moment in the text. The cross begins to loom more largely over the narrative, and Mark's already rapid pace picks up to breakneck speed toward Calvary. Therefore:

> [H]e began to teach them that the Son of Man must suffer many things and be rejected by the elders and the chief priests and the scribes and be killed, and after three days rise again. And he said this plainly. And Peter took him aside and began to rebuke him. (vv. 31–32)

This is not how Peter has heard about the Messiah's coming. Somehow Isaiah 53 and Psalm 22 have slipped through the cracks; rather, the Messiah is supposed to come and overthrow the oppressors, to restore earthly order through military force, swords and banners waving. This whole "Messiah dying" thing? No way.

> But turning and seeing his disciples, he rebuked Peter and said, "Get behind me, Satan! For you are not setting your mind on the things of God, but on the things of man." (Mark 8:33)

So often we try to have Jesus without his cross. We carry on, assuming the Christian life should be typified by comfort rather than suffering, assuming sin will disappear without its being intentionally killed, assuming Jesus saves us because we're essentially awesome people.

But the Savior without the cross is no Savior. The Messiah without the cross is no Messiah. The King without the cross is no King. So to take Jesus and remove the offense of the cross is a satanic act. When you seek to have Christ without taking his cross, you are not aligning with Christ but with the Devil.

Matthew 7:21–23 tells us that at the end of days, there will be many who basically say to Jesus: "Lord, Lord, did we not cast out demons in your name? Did we not do good works in your name? Did we not claim to follow you? Did we not say we loved you? Did we not go to church? Did we not vote for Christians in elections? Did we not listen to Christian radio stations? Did we not own Bibles?" And Jesus will say to them, "Depart from me, I never knew you."

Why? Because they sought to have Jesus without his cross.

Some will say, "Oh, no, no, I know Jesus died on the cross for me." But the problem is that they will never have died with him (Rom. 6:6; Gal. 2:20; 6:14).

Jesus gives his disciples a flash-forward moment, a glimpse into the depths of his incarnational ministry. And it is frightening:

And calling the crowd to him with his disciples, he said to them, "If anyone would come after me, let him deny himself and take up his cross and follow me. For whoever would save his life will lose it, but whoever loses his life for my sake and the gospel's will save it." (Mark 8:34–35)

See, God is not looking for a new PR firm. He's not looking for fans. He's not looking for people to wear the club T-shirt. He's looking for men and women willing to die to their old way of life—the way that leads to death—and follow him to his cross, the way that leads to life.

Your reaction to Christ directly results from just how saving you see him to be. If all you see are the wonders but not the wonder worker, you are missing the only vision necessary for salvation.

Mark 8 makes it clear that we can look without seeing. But we cannot see without looking, so let's keep looking! As Ray Ortlund says, "Stare at the glory of God until you see it."

And there is more to see still in Jesus's healing of the blind.

## Measure Twice, Cut Once

The stakes cannot get any higher. It is crucial that we sort out the spiritual matters as quickly as possible to become as secure as possible. The story of the healing of the man born blind in John 9 supports that important lesson. An inaccurate vision can be eternally disastrous:

> As he passed by, he saw a man blind from birth. And his disciples asked him, "Rabbi, who sinned, this man or his parents, that he was born blind?" Jesus answered, "It was not that this man sinned, or his parents, but that the works of God might be displayed in him. We must work the works of him who sent me while it is day; night is coming, when no one can work. As long as I am in the world, I am the light of the world." Having said these things, he spit on the ground and made mud with the saliva. Then he anointed the man's eyes with the mud and said to him, "Go, wash in the pool of Siloam" (which means Sent). So he went and washed and came back seeing. (John 9:1–7)

As I've said previously, every healing of the blind in the Gospels accompanies a doctrinal message. In this story, the teaching of Jesus dismantles the spiritual economy of the self-righteous.

The Bible makes it very clear that the reason there are diseases and disabilities in the world is sin. The world is broken because of sin. But this is not the same thing as saying that a particular person's disease or disability is directly the result of his personal sin. In other words, someone's suffering from brain cancer is the consequence of living in a fallen world, but it is not the consequence of his personal sin. In John 9:2, the disciples appear to subscribe to some kind of karmic view of God's creation or some proto-prosperity gospel. The man was born blind as punishment for someone's sin, they reason. They cannot help but think in terms of the scorecard. In life, there are winners and losers.

But this is not the game Jesus plays. It is certainly not the spiritual economy of the kingdom. Jesus's Sermon on the Mount is enough evidence against that. Look primarily at the Beatitudes. Jesus tears up the scorecard and declares us all losers. And the winners, he proclaims, are those who are willing to admit they're losers.

People are not born with diseases and disabilities so that we are able to determine who's in and who's out, who's good and who's bad, who's clean and who's unclean. They are born with such afflictions as a reminder of everyone's sin and therefore everyone's need. (Really, when we see a person suffering from a disease or disability, we should feel convicted of our own sin.) And this healing in John 9 is a reminder that real healing comes not through our goodness but God's. To prove this point, Jesus makes a mess of dirt and spit, and uses it to heal the man of his blindness.

Once again, we encounter an echo of the creation in this act of new creation. The merging of the dust of the ground and the expectoration of the divine results in life. In Jesus's miracles, we see an image of him making all things new.

The Pharisees in particular have a huge problem with this whole thing. John 9 goes on to recount how they interact with the man healed from his blindness, drag his parents into the mess, and eventually confront Jesus himself, to which Jesus responds:

> "For judgment I came into this world, that those who do not see may see, and those who see may become blind." Some of the Pharisees near him heard these things, and said to him, "Are we also blind?" Jesus said to them, "If you were blind,

you would have no guilt; but now that you say, 'We see,' your guilt remains." (vv. 39–41)

The Pharisees' vision is very poor. They look at themselves and see people who quite clearly measure up. They look at Jesus and see a person who clearly does not. In each estimation, they are way, way off.

Jesus commands them to get their measurements right. Before they start making determinations of who's in and who's out, they ought to make sure they've accurately run the numbers. If they properly measure themselves, they will see that they are spiritually blind. And if they properly measure Jesus, they will see that he is the light of the world with measureless glory. And until you and I can see those two things, we will never see.

## The True Vision of Glory

Most of us fill our visions with ourselves. We find ourselves exceptionally glorious, don't we? Through understanding of the Scriptures, we ought to see that this vision is dangerous and silly. When we are captivated with the vision of us, even our attempts to serve Jesus get mucked up with self-interest and vainglory.

This is perhaps nowhere more clear in the Bible than in the story of the healing of blind Bartimaeus. That story begins before it begins, though, as Mark wisely connects it to the arrogant request of James and John:

> And they were on the road, going up to Jerusalem, and Jesus was walking ahead of them. And they were amazed, and those who followed were afraid. And taking the twelve again, he began to tell them what was to happen to him, saying, "See, we are going up to Jerusalem, and the Son of Man will be delivered over to the chief priests and the scribes, and they will condemn him to death and deliver him over to the Gentiles. And they will mock him and spit on him, and flog him and kill him. And after three days he will rise." (Mark 10:32–34)

One thing I love about this passage is that the disciples are scared—and Jesus tells them a scary story. Jesus certainly doesn't mollycoddle his followers! He's not our mama. He's not there to say everything's going to be okay. Some things will not be okay. So we can always count on Jesus to be totally honest.

Now, if you pair what takes place immediately before this in Jesus's encounter with the rich young ruler (vv. 17–31) with the sobering pronouncement Jesus now makes, what happens next is that much more galling:

> And James and John, the sons of Zebedee, came up to him and said to him, "Teacher, we want you to do for us whatever we ask of you." And he said to them, "What do you want me to do for you?" (vv. 35–36)

I assume the look on Jesus's face communicates, "This oughta be good."

Matthew's account (20:20–28) has their mother making the request. I can't figure out whether, by leaving this detail out, Peter (through Mark) is trying to make them look better or worse. I assume better.

> And they said to him, "Grant us to sit, one at your right hand and one at your left, in your glory." (Mark 10:37)

We understand this request as terrible right away. It is prideful; it is confused. What we don't often recognize right away is that it is emblematic of so many of our own requests, indeed of our entire life mission. All of us are, in our own ways, quite taken with our own ambitious yearnings for self-fulfillment. And in our flesh, we always want the glory without the cross.

> Jesus said to them, "You do not know what you are asking. Are you able to drink the cup that I drink, or to be baptized with the baptism with which I am baptized?" And they said to him, "We are able." And Jesus said to them, "The cup that

I drink you will drink, and with the baptism with which I am baptized, you will be baptized, but to sit at my right hand or at my left is not mine to grant, but it is for those for whom it has been prepared." (vv. 38–40)

The cup Jesus is referring to here is undoubtedly the cup of God's wrath. He is speaking of the same death he has just told them he must endure. In other words, Jesus is trying to cut through their hazy vision of personal victory and promotion. "I didn't come to hand out medals and trophies, brothers, but crosses."

We must get this straight or we will never understand Christianity. Always at the center of Christianity is the death of Christ. His death is our life. We are always trying to run an end-around past the cross, to cut through the temple on our way to glory without minding the sacrifice.

Paul elaborates on this dysfunction of vision this way:

For the word of the cross is folly to those who are perishing, but to us who are being saved it is the power of God. For it is written,

"I will destroy the wisdom of the wise,
and the discernment of the discerning I will thwart."

Where is the one who is wise? Where is the scribe? Where is the debater of this age? Has not God made foolish the wisdom of the world? For since, in the wisdom of God, the world did not know God through wisdom, it pleased God through the folly of what we preach to save those who believe. For Jews demand signs and Greeks seek wisdom, but we preach Christ crucified, a stumbling block to Jews and folly to Gentiles, but to those who are called, both Jews and Greeks, Christ the power of God and the wisdom of God. For the foolishness of God is wiser than men, and the weakness of God is stronger than men. (1 Cor. 1:18–25)

When we see the cross of Christ, in fact, we tend to react in one of two ways: aversion or affection. What makes the difference is what we expect from Jesus: congratulations or grace.

James and John are jockeying for position. They see the writing on the wall and want to make sure they get theirs. But to jockey for position, to seek to "get yours," to look first for glory without the cross is to be shriveled down to darkest nothing. To press into the dark death at the center of the cross, however, is to come out in the expansive, unconquerable glory of resurrection and renewal.

The vision the disciples have is for their own exaltation. They see themselves. So they reveal their blindness. By contrast, look at what happens next:

> And they came to Jericho. And as he was leaving Jericho with his disciples and a great crowd, Bartimaeus, a blind beggar, the son of Timaeus, was sitting by the roadside. And when he heard that it was Jesus of Nazareth, he began to cry out and say, "Jesus, Son of David, have mercy on me!" And many rebuked him, telling him to be silent. But he cried out all the more, "Son of David, have mercy on me!" And Jesus stopped and said, "Call him." And they called the blind man, saying to him, "Take heart. Get up; he is calling you." And throwing off his cloak, he sprang up and came to Jesus. And Jesus said to him, "What do you want me to do for you?" And the blind man said to him, "Rabbi, let me recover my sight." And Jesus said to him, "Go your way; your faith has made you well." And immediately he recovered his sight and followed him on the way. (Mark 10:46–52)

Notice the similarities between this exchange and the one between Jesus and the sons of Zebedee. And in the similarities, notice the contrast. There are two requests across both stories: "Do for us whatever we want" versus "Have mercy on me!" (or, in other words, "Do whatever *you* want!").

Jesus responds to both with the same question: "What do you want me to do for you?"

James and John shoot for the moon. They figure they deserve it. Bartimaeus is thinking in terms not of merit but need: "I just want to see."

When we come to Christ for congratulations, we see the cross with aversion. When we come for grace, we see the cross with affection.

When we can't see Christ, we can't see that the things we want don't ultimately satisfy. And we can't see why they don't satisfy.

My absolute all-time favorite athlete is New England Patriots quarterback Tom Brady. I like watching Brady play football so out of proportion that it's comical. Most of my friends and family make fun of me. And while I enjoy playing along by playing into their accusations about my "man crush" on the man, I admit, without any joke, that Brady's play makes me very happy. But what makes me very sad is contemplating the *60 Minutes* interview of Brady by CBS's Steve Kroft a few years back.

Brady said: "Why do I have three Super Bowl rings and still think there's something greater out there for me? I mean, maybe a lot of people would say, 'Hey man, this is what is.' I reached my goal, my dream, my life. Me, I think, 'God, it's got to be more than this.' I mean this isn't, this can't be what it's all cracked up to be."

Kroft asked him, "What's the answer?"

Brady responded: "I wish I knew. I wish I knew. I love playing football and I love being quarterback for this team. But at the same time, I think there are a lot of other parts about me that I'm trying to find."

This is profoundly sad. And what strikes me in the quarterback's words is that he doesn't say, "I think there are lots of other parts about life I'm trying to find," but that there are lots of other parts about "me" he's trying to find. The man appears to be looking into himself to satisfy the eternal longing in his heart. But emptiness cannot fill emptiness.

One of the great things about Brady's legacy is the way he was so often second-guessed by his college coaches and even NFL scouts. There is a now-infamous photo of young Brady at the NFL Scouting Combine, standing forlornly in athletic shorts and no shirt. He is not obviously muscular. He is pasty, lanky, and fairly, well, *goofy-looking*, actually. He is hardly the specimen of athletic perfection. But he has succeeded far beyond previous expectations and is regarded by many as not just one of the greatest quarterbacks but the greatest quarterback. This is partly because Brady has an uncanny ability to process at the line of scrimmage. He has what they call "a football brain." He can read defenses very quickly, within seconds, and releases the ball with lightning speed and laser-like precision. See, lots of quarterbacks see the defense. But Brady *sees* the defense.

Oh, Lord, help Tom not to simply see the cross but to *see* the cross.

It is as if James and John have finally received their promotion and have to ask, "Is this it?"

Brady, despite his riches, fame, acclaim, and success, may be much closer to salvation, given his confession. The real danger is for those who get everything they ever really wanted and feel satisfied. It is perhaps a modern myth of the church that every lost person feels lost. The reality for many of us is that we are too satisfied with our ambitions. That is a scary place to be.

There is seeing and then there's *seeing*. There is a vision of intellect, of nature, of the flesh. And then there's the vision gathered with the spiritual senses, the part of us that is dead until raised by the Spirit himself.

The Lord must make us see. We cannot see otherwise. The blind do not heal themselves.

So when our hearts are broken, our strength is failing, we feel alone, and all the things we've asked God for that aren't eternal show their temporariness, let us remember to look up to the Lord on high and say, "Have mercy on me."

That's a request Christ always grants. He has the authority to serve you by saving you from your sin and your stupid requests. If you have the humility to ask for nothing but mercy to see him, nothing but glory awaits.

The story of Charles Spurgeon's conversion captures the difference between seeing and *seeing* quite well:

> I sometimes think I might have been in darkness and despair until now had it not been for the goodness of God in sending a snowstorm, one Sunday morning, while I was going to a certain place of worship. When I could go no further, I turned down a side street, and came to a little Primitive Methodist Chapel. In that chapel there may have been a dozen or fifteen people. . . . The minister did not come that morning; he was snowed up, I suppose. At last, a very thin-looking man, a shoemaker, or tailor, or something of that sort, went up into the pulpit to preach. . . . He was obliged to stick to his text, for the simple reason that he had little else to say. The text was
>
> "LOOK UNTO ME, AND BE YE SAVED, ALL THE ENDS OF THE EARTH." [Isa. 45:22].
>
> He did not even pronounce the words rightly, but that did not matter. There was, I thought, a glimpse of hope for me in that text. The preacher began thus:—"My dear friends, this is a very simple text indeed. It says, 'Look.' Now lookin' don't take a deal of pains. It ain't liftin' your foot or your finger; it is just, 'Look.' Well, a man needn't go to College to learn to look. You may be the biggest fool, and yet you can look. A man needn't be worth a thousand a year to be able to look. Anyone can look; even a child can look. But then the text says, 'Look unto *Me*.' . . . [M]any of ye are lookin' to yourselves, but it's no use lookin' there. You'll never find any comfort in yourselves. Some look to God the Father. No, look to Him by-and-by. Jesus Christ says, 'Look unto *Me*.' Some of ye say, 'We must wait for the Spirit's workin'.' You have no business with that just now. Look to Christ. The text says, 'Look unto Me.'"
>
> Then the good man followed up his text in this way:— "Look unto Me; I am sweatin' great drops of blood. Look unto Me; I am hangin' on the cross. Look unto Me; I am dead and buried. Look unto Me; I rise again. Look unto Me; I ascend to

heaven. Look unto Me; I am sittin' at the Father's right hand. O poor sinner, look unto Me! Look unto Me!"

When he had gone to about that length, and managed to spin out ten minutes or so, he was at the end of his tether. Then he looked at me under the gallery, and I daresay, with so few present, he knew me to be a stranger. Just fixing his eyes on me, as if he knew all my heart, he said, "Young man, you look very miserable." Well, I did; but I had not been accustomed to have remarks made from the pulpit on my personal appearance before. However, it was a good blow, struck right home. He continued, "and you always will be miserable—miserable in life, and miserable in death,—if you don't obey my text; but if you obey now, this moment, you will be saved." Then, lifting up his hands, he shouted, as only a Primitive Methodist could do, "Young man, look to Jesus Christ. Look! Look! Look! You have nothin' to do but to look and live." I saw at once the way of salvation. I know not what else he said,—I did not take much notice of it,—I was so possessed with that one thought. Like as when the brazen serpent was lifted up, the people only looked and were healed, so it was with me. I had been waiting to do fifty things, but when I heard that word, "Look!" what a charming word it seemed to me! Oh! I looked until I could have almost looked my eyes away. There and then the cloud was gone, the darkness had rolled away, and that moment I saw the sun; and I could have risen that instant, and sung with the most enthusiastic of them, of the precious blood of Christ, and the simple faith which looks alone to Him. . . . [A]nd now I can say,—

E'er since by faith I saw the stream
Your flowing wounds supply,
Redeeming love has been my theme,
And shall be till I die."[1]

---

[1] Charles Haddon Spurgeon, *The Autobiography of Charles H. Spurgeon*, vol. 1: 1834–1854 (Chicago: Fleming H. Revell, 1898), 105–8. The poem stanza Spurgeon cites is from the hymn "There Is a Fountain Filled with Blood" by William Cowper (1771).

From the mere speaking of the word of the gospel, the Spirit's power was in full effect, raising the shades over Spurgeon's heart. The sunlight streamed in and the darkness was vanquished. Climactically he looked, and he *saw*.

In Matthew 12:22, we read, "Then a demon-oppressed man who was blind and mute was brought to him, and he healed him, so that the man spoke and saw."

Here the disability of the man is implicitly attributed to demonic oppression. This is not always (or even usually) the cause of physical ailments, but the connection is made here so that we may see Christ's kingdom-shaking force in stark display. For Christ to make the blind see, the mute speak, the deaf hear, the lame walk, and the sick restored is to say, "I am in charge and death's reign is over."

And if Christ is in charge, pretenders to the throne, no matter how powerful or convincing, will be crushed.

# 7

# The Conquest of the Dark Domain

So much of the satanic realm is hidden from our view, and this is probably a very good thing. Curious minds such as ours, drawn to knowledge we shouldn't have, knowledge we could do nothing good with, would be tempted greatly to unhealthy fixation. God therefore obscures many details in the Scriptures about the origins of the Devil. What has been revealed has given rise to a great deal of speculation, however, and it can sometimes be difficult in the popular evangelical imagination to determine where the Bible ends and John Milton (or Frank Peretti) begins.

Second Peter 2:4 informs us that demons are angels who "sinned." Jude 6 refers to them as "angels who did not stay within their own position of authority." Some see the fall of Satan from heaven in the taunting of Babylon in Isaiah 14.

The Devil shows up very early in the story of the kingdom. He is present in the garden, scheming against God's good creation. And his designs against the beloved children of God are successful. But his victory is very short-lived. He is cursed alongside the first couple and with creation:

> The LORD God said to the serpent,
>
> "Because you have done this,
>     cursed are you above all livestock

and above all beasts of the field;
on your belly you shall go,
and dust you shall eat
all the days of your life." (Gen. 3:14)

If any passage of Scripture may serve as evidence that God and the Devil are not locked in some intractable balance of Tao-esque good and evil, like yin to the other's yang, this one, wherein we see God make the Serpent eat his dust forever, ought to do it.

But we also see Satan needing permission from God to do his tempting (Job 1:6–12). And in that original curse, we see the "first gospel":

I will put enmity between you and the woman,
    and between your offspring and her offspring;
he shall bruise your head,
    and you shall bruise his heel. (Gen. 3:15)

The Devil's got an expiration date. He is no match for the King, and every power he wields is granted, allowed for the moment. The Lord's got the Devil on a leash, and when Jesus comes announcing the kingdom, he begins shortening the chain.

There is a well-worn rule of playwriting that goes like this: if you introduce a gun in the first act, it must get fired in the last. And because God is an excellent storyteller, what has been suggested in the first act (Gen. 3:15) shows up in the last:

And he seized the dragon, that ancient serpent, who is the devil and Satan, and bound him for a thousand years. . . . [A]nd the devil who had deceived them was thrown into the lake of fire and sulfur where the beast and the false prophet were, and they will be tormented day and night forever and ever. (Rev. 20:2, 10)

This is why I believe the end times begin with Jesus: as soon as he shows up, he begins this long-foretold, inevitable conquest.

John tells us straightaway, "The light shines in the darkness, and the darkness has not overcome it" (John 1:5). And Mark's Gospel highlights Jesus's assault on the demonic domain (1:21–28) immediately after the call of the disciples. Later, the disciples come to Jesus, marveling that they are able to cast out demons, too. Jesus responds:

> I saw Satan fall like lightning from heaven. Behold, I have given you authority to tread on serpents and scorpions, and over all the power of the enemy, and nothing shall hurt you. (Luke 10:18–19)

It is tempting to read Jesus's words here as hyperbole, but while he is not saying his disciples are now omnipotent—remember, later they have trouble casting out a particularly pernicious demon (Mark 9:18, 28–29)—this is the same King who will tell his subjects with a straight face that "everyone who lives and believes in me shall never die" (John 11:26). He is saying, without exaggeration, that to lay hold of the kingdom is to lay hold of an enormous spiritual power straight from heaven, a power that the Devil and his demons must submit to.

Can this be? The coming of the kingdom in and through Jesus turns the tables on that old snake. The tempted have the tempter by the tail now. If we resist him, he will flee like the whipped dog he is (James 4:7). What an amazing development in the story of good and evil! It seems as though even the weakest faith can now move mountains, can make them, in fact, fall right onto the heads of demons. The Savior has inexplicably given sinners access to his royal scepter that they might smash the head of the Serpent with it.

## The All-Conquering Faith of the Inglorious Sinner

In Mark 9, Jesus takes Peter, James, and John up a mountain to witness a revelation of his divine glory. We call this event the transfiguration, and there will be a more extensive discussion of it in chapter 10. Left behind during this episode are the other nine disciples, however, and when Jesus and the three return from the mountain, they come upon the group suffering the slings and arrows of outraged forces:

> And when they came to the disciples, they saw a great crowd around them, and scribes arguing with them. And immediately all the crowd, when they saw him, were greatly amazed and ran up to him and greeted him. And he asked them, "What are you arguing about with them?" And someone from the crowd answered him, "Teacher, I brought my son to you, for he has a spirit that makes him mute. And whenever it seizes him, it throws him down, and he foams and grinds his teeth and becomes rigid. So I asked your disciples to cast it out, and they were not able." (vv. 14–18)

It is curious that the father of the boy answers the question apparently addressed to the disciples. It is possible that the argument is actually about the boy's exorcism, especially given the later context of the disciples' question.

The child suffers from what sounds like epilepsy, but here it is attributed to an unclean spirit. The people of Jesus's day did not always equate sickness with demonic oppression; they were religious but not as superstitious as we moderns like to think. They may not have been medically advanced, but they were generally able to discern the difference between bodily ailments and demonic activity, especially when the activity included strange voices, extraordinary strength, and, in the case of this young victim, throwing himself into fire and water. There is a definite malice involved in his affliction.

Jesus's response is interesting, to say the least:

> O faithless generation, how long am I to be with you? How long am I to bear with you? Bring him to me. (v. 19)

The Lord's lament is likely a reflection of his being overwhelmed by the burden of each part of the crowd. The father has come looking for help, but he carries with him a doubt that Jesus is already discerning. The disciples are constantly slow to learn and to trust, even though they are constantly exposed to the glory of the Lord in word and deed. The scribes, of course, are a stubborn presence with their continual arguing and challenging.

> And they brought the boy to him. And when the spirit saw him, immediately it convulsed the boy, and he fell on the ground and rolled about, foaming at the mouth. (v. 20)

This is another indication that we are reading of demonic possession and not simply an epileptic seizure. The very sight of Jesus makes the demons shudder.

> And Jesus asked his father, "How long has this been happening to him?" And he said, "From childhood. And it has often cast him into fire and into water, to destroy him. But if you can do anything, have compassion on us and help us." And Jesus said to him, "'If you can'! All things are possible for one who believes." (vv. 21–23)

At this point, it is important to know just what faith is.

When Jesus says, "All things are possible for one who believes," does he mean that a five-year-old can dunk a basketball if he just sincerely believes he can? (Does he mean that any more than he means in Mark 16:18 that they are welcome to start those snake-handling churches we hear so much about in Appalachia?) As I write this, social media has been fleetingly agog over Nik Wallenda's crossing of the Grand Canyon on a tightrope, sans net and tether. Wallenda is a Christian, and his faith is apparently very important to his stunts. Or so we are being told on Twitter, where Philippians 4:13 has been wielded so liberally it has nearly lost all sense. Is tightrope walking what Paul is talking about in Philippians 4:13? Would that verse be any less true if Wallenda had fallen off the rope to his death?

No, faith is not a rabbit's foot. Hebrews 11:1 tells us that "faith is the assurance of things hoped for, the conviction of things not seen." Faith is a nonempirical trust. In the context of the Scriptures, faith is a trust, despite all visible evidence to the contrary, that based on all the spiritual evidence, Jesus Christ is exactly who he says he is and will do all he says he will.

Faith is an empty vessel. It's an open hand. It's an openness to be filled with Jesus. When we come to Christ in faith, we are saying, "I need you and I want you; therefore, I trust you to save me eternally." Don't bring any works. That's not an empty hand. Don't bring a sense of righteousness. That's not an empty hand. Bring your messed-up, broken, sinful self. Jesus came only to save sinners. If you're not a sinner, you can't have Jesus.

So, "all things are possible for one who believes" isn't some inspirational, self-helpy Dr. Phil "keep your New Year's resolutions" mantra. It is a promise that trusters in Christ will not be conquered.

Jesus's retort to the father, "If you can!" may be read more along the lines of "Now, about that 'if you can'—if you would trust me, you would know there is no limit to what I can do."

Because Jesus conquers all things, faith then conquers all things.

Because faith conquers all things, it conquers the law. We can't do that on our own. Jesus's perfect righteousness does it for us, but we are able to do it vicariously through him because he died vicariously for us and thus satisfied the law's demands on our behalf. It was Abraham's faith, remember, that was credited to him as righteousness, not his good works (Rom. 4:9).

Because faith is the empty vessel filled with Christ, it conquers sin. We can't do that on our own. But Jesus nails sin to the cross, and because his death becomes our death through faith, his power over sin becomes our power over sin through faith.

Because faith is the empty vessel filled with Christ, it conquers death. We can't do that on our own. But Jesus rises again, and because his resurrection becomes our resurrection through faith, his power over death becomes our power over death through faith.

Because faith is the empty vessel filled with Christ, it conquers any stressful, terrifying, or trying situation. Left alone, we are anxious, fearful, stressed. But remembering that Jesus is everything and that to have him makes us loved, justified, secured, and satisfied means not only that we can "be anxious for nothing" (Phil. 4:6, NKJV) but that we can "rejoice always" (1 Thess. 5:16).

Faith conquers everything.

Now, about that whole "if he can" stuff . . .

## Faith Conquers Doubt

> Immediately the father of the child cried out and said, "I believe; help my unbelief!" (Mark 9:24)

What this man says is deeply profound, probably without his even knowing it. He is putting the whole of Romans 7 into one desperate exclamation.

Because Jesus justifies us, we are welcome and empowered then to be honest about our struggles. We have nothing left to prove or hide. There is mercy for God's doubting children, so long as there is an overarching "I believe" to the daily prayer "help my unbelief."

From conversion throughout our progressive sanctification, our prayer may be that the Lord will help us press belief into every corner of our hearts, into every gap in our lives. The gospel goes on taking dominion over us, even as it has already staked its claim on us forever. We are, then, daily working out what God has worked in us (Phil. 2:12–13).

Life is filled with doubting moments. And we must be honest, not just about our doubts but about what doubt is. The Bible says to treat doubters with mercy (Jude 22), but it never says a kind thing about doubt itself.

Doubt is seeded by the Devil himself. Every doubting of any aspect of Christ's goodness and grace is a reverberation of that first temptation question, "Did God actually say . . . ?" (Gen. 3:1). Therefore, "I believe; help my unbelief!" is spiritual warfare.

May I offer a few ways to believe by battling unbelief?

*First, concentrate on the historical fact of the cross.* Following

Christ's concession to Thomas (John 20:27), press into Jesus's wounds. Read the Gospel accounts of the passion. Read scholarly works about the cross. Reflect intellectually and devotionally on what the man Jesus of Nazareth did and why he did it.

*Second, do not seek refuge or advice with those who would shame you for doubting—as if they never do.* We doubters need gospel, not law. So seek out community that neither allows you to coddle your doubt nor treats you as if doubt is the unpardonable sin.

*Third, pray.* "The apostles said to the Lord, 'Increase our faith!'" (Luke 17:5). You may doubt God is there or doubt his love for you, but as a combative measure against the discomfort of doubt, push back, and act as if he is there and that he does love you. Throw yourself at him. Cry out to him honestly and humbly. If you approach the throne boldly, you will find grace there for your time of need.

*Fourth, refocus your doubts toward your own failings and inability.* Doubt yourself, in other words. Doubt your doubts. This is counterintuitive to some, and it sounds like bad advice in this age of "Believe in yourself," self-help, and the therapeutic gospel of human potential, but we will not believe God more fully until we despair of ourselves more fully.

In this sense, the counterattack is not to "stop doubting God"—which may be much like telling a drowning man to thrash harder—but to start doubting yourself. It is telling a drowning man to stop thrashing, to doubt his own ability to thrash his way to safety. In fact, when a drowning man relaxes and stops fighting, giving up trust in his ability to save himself, his rescuer is better able to swim him to safety.

If you think God can't be trusted, think about yourself. How together are *you*? How well do you have it figured out? How in control are you? How are your plans coming together for a great life? How is "following your heart," which is "deceitful above all things" (Jer. 17:9), working out for you?

If we are honest with ourselves, we realize our utter dependence and feebleness. And when we doubt ourselves, we are ready to trust God, becoming less as he becomes greater (John 3:30).

*Finally, read your Bible.* More specifically, meditate on scriptural promises related to your area of doubt.

Your doubt will wither and fade, but the Word of the Lord lasts forever. Remember that God is bigger than your doubt, that your "disagreement" with your doubt is an indication you are known by him. Remember that Christ's perfect work covers even our wavering faith. You need only a mustard seed.

I've heard Matt Chandler say that when he was lost, he had a lot of questions about Christianity, but God saved him without answering any of them. How can this be? He heard the gospel, he says.

We tend to see faith as this wobbly thing, when really it is doubt that is wobbly: "But let him ask in faith, with no doubting, for the one who doubts is like a wave of the sea that is driven and tossed by the wind" (James 1:6).

Doubt comes in when faith does not seem sufficient for the job. We want more. We want results. We want empirical certainty. But Christ fills faith, not simply intellect. The demons "know" Jesus is Lord. But they don't trust him. The reality, of course, is that ultimately even our faith is not unreasonable. But neither is it reason. Faith is not irrational, but it is not rationalism.

But the more you trust, the more you see that Christ proves himself worthy and the easier it becomes to pray more and more, "Lord, I believe; help my unbelief." The all-conquering Christ of faith day by day removes all doubt.

## Faith Conquers Hell

Here is the bottom line: the promise that we will not fall below the eternal bottom line. Jesus holds us up. Peter confesses that Jesus Christ is Lord. This is a statement of pure, childlike faith, and Jesus says not even hell itself can conquer the kingdom built on it (Matt. 16:16–18). Peter's confession speaks to Christ's hell-proof, hell-conquering kingdom, the kingdom that announces freedom

for those in bondage to the enemy and his infernal minions, like
the possessed boy in Mark 9.

> And when Jesus saw that a crowd came running together, he
> rebuked the unclean spirit, saying to it, "You mute and deaf
> spirit, I command you, come out of him and never enter him
> again." And after crying out and convulsing him terribly, it
> came out, and the boy was like a corpse, so that most of them
> said, "He is dead." But Jesus took him by the hand and lifted
> him up, and he arose. (Mark 9:25–27)

"And he arose." There are shades of resurrection here. The domain of death is being dismantled, stone by stone. The infernal
kingdom is being plundered. Its captives are being freed.

Where all else fails, including our best religious efforts, Jesus
never fails.

> And when he had entered the house, his disciples asked
> him privately, "Why could we not cast it out?" And he said
> to them, "This kind cannot be driven out by anything but
> prayer." (vv. 28–29)

Prayer is a living parable of faith because it presupposes helplessness. When we pray, we are acknowledging that we do not
have the power to accomplish whatever we are bringing before
the Lord. (Conversely, when we are not praying, it is because we
are essentially believing, "I've got this one.") Prayer is the deepest
act of faith, particularly if we pray as Jesus did, "Not my will, but
yours, be done" (Luke 22:42).

Jesus explains the difficulty of this exorcism by revealing the
disciples' lack of prayer. I think it's not incidental that this lesson
on faith comes in the context of a story of demon possession, because it helps us see that times of doubting the Lord's goodness and
the gospel are seeded by the Devil's accusations. That voice that
says, "Oh, this isn't true"? That's demonic.

But the faith that prayer and fasting evince disrupts the jurisdiction of the Devil and conquers hell itself. Why? Because faith is the empty vessel that Christ fills, and Christ conquers hell. Sydney Page writes:

> Mark focuses on the need for prayer because it clearly demonstrates that divine power is not under human control; it must always be asked for. Manifestations of the power of God, such as are needed when dealing with the forces of evil, come only in response to the attitude of trust and reliance upon God that is expressed in humble prayer.[1]

We cannot conquer the power of hell ourselves. It subdues us, subsumes us. Faith alone is our victory, because faith is filled with the Victor.

## On the Right Side of Victory

"He has sent me to proclaim liberty to the captives," Jesus says in Luke 4:18, quoting Isaiah 61:1. The gospel of the kingdom is that prisoners to the forces of evil are being set free left and right. Jesus sets prisoners free from the bondage of physical afflictions, as we see in the deliverance of the boy in Mark 9. Jesus sets prisoners free from the bondage of emotional afflictions and physical oppression, as we see in his vanquishing of Legion from the Gerasene (Mark 5:1–20). Jesus even sets prisoners free from the bondage of religious ethnocentrism, as we see when he exorcises the demon from the Syrophoenician woman's daughter (Mark 7:24–30).

Everywhere he goes, Jesus draws a line in the spiritual sand and, in the magnificent magnetism of his ministry, creates separation between those who love him and those who oppose him. The sheer divisiveness of Jesus and his kingdom is clear in statements such as "No servant can serve two masters" (Luke 16:13) and "Whoever is not with me is against me" (Matt. 12:30). The kingdom division is undeniable in Matthew 10:34–37:

---

[1] Sydney H. T. Page, *Powers of Evil: A Biblical Study of Satan and Demons* (Grand Rapids, MI: Baker, 1995), 164.

> Do not think that I have come to bring peace to the earth. I have not come to bring peace, but a sword. For I have come to set a man against his father, and a daughter against her mother, and a daughter-in-law against her mother-in-law. And a person's enemies will be those of his own household. Whoever loves father or mother more than me is not worthy of me, and whoever loves son or daughter more than me is not worthy of me.

Jesus is not forming a fan club. He is demanding allegiance.

We see the crucial character of kingdom divisiveness in Jesus's teaching on spiritual warfare in Mark 3. Jesus's family is concerned for him (vv. 21, 31–35)—whether for his safety or for his sanity we can't be too sure, but perhaps it's a little of both. Certainly the social guardians of the day are concerned about him, if not for him, as they oppose him at every turn. The sword of his authority makes several cuts in Mark 3. Let us look at his defense of his exorcisms first:

> And the scribes who came down from Jerusalem were saying, "He is possessed by Beelzebul," and "by the prince of demons he casts out the demons." And he called them to him and said to them in parables, "How can Satan cast out Satan? If a kingdom is divided against itself, that kingdom cannot stand. And if a house is divided against itself, that house will not be able to stand. And if Satan has risen up against himself and is divided, he cannot stand, but is coming to an end. But no one can enter a strong man's house and plunder his goods, unless he first binds the strong man. Then indeed he may plunder his house. (3:22–27)

As we've said, Jesus's family is concerned about him, but the scribes who have come down from Jerusalem flat-out hate Jesus. They are accusing him here of working his miracles by the power of Beelzebul, the "lord of the flies," who is Satan. This is not just a bit of confusion or misunderstanding, but a deliberate misinterpretation. Faced with Jesus's power and growth, they assert that his kingdom is satanic. This is no isolated incident, as we read in John 10:20: "Many of them said, 'He has a demon, and is insane; why listen to him?'"

Jesus's reference to "a house divided against itself" must have the issues related to his own family in the background. They try to stop his ministry (Mark 3:21). Later, they appeal to him once again to cease his provocation (vv. 31–35). Jesus may be answering the spiritual warfare question about his demonic exorcisms, but he is also answering the spiritual warfare question about discipleship to him in general.

Mark says the answer is a parable, but it is certainly one of the clearest to interpret. In a mix of sarcasm and sheer logic, Jesus highlights the nonsensicalness of Satan casting himself out. He has employed this kind of absurd exaggeration to highlight error quite a bit.

- Which good work are you stoning me for? (John 10:32)
- It's easier for a camel to jump through a needle's eye than for a rich man to enter heaven. (Mark 10:25)
- Do you buy lamps to put under the bed? (Luke 8:16)

In the parallels to this exchange (Matt. 12:22–32; Luke 11:14–23), Jesus asks his interlocutors, "If I cast out demons by the Devil, whom do your sons use?"

In today's parlance, the sarcasm of Jesus's response might be paraphrased this way: "Right, you morons, Satan is casting out Satan. That makes total sense. Because he's trying to lose." If you think this is mean, you should know that it gets worse. In Proverbs 26:3, we read that the back of a fool needs a rod, and Jesus is here giving these fools a rhetorical whipping. He is trying, in fact, to startle them sober, so they'll really hear what he says next: "none can enter a strong man's house and plunder his goods, unless he first binds the strong man. Then indeed he may plunder his house" (Mark 3:27).

Jesus's conquest is Satan's defeat. And to the victor go the spoils.

Approximately one thousand years earlier, a shepherd from Bethlehem found his family and friends shaking at the terror and might of the enemy. A line had been drawn and opposing forces gathered. The situation looked hopeless for good. The prospects for evil seemed glorious. But the shepherd boy confronted the enemy's fiercest warrior and took him out with one stone. Then he sliced his head off with his own sword and treated it like a trophy, signaling to his people that the enemy's reign was over. In jubilation, then, the forces of good stormed the enemy camp, plundering its goods (1 Sam. 17:53). The strong man had been bound for good. All his stuff was now up for grabs.

In Revelation 20:1–2 we read:

> Then I saw an angel coming down from heaven, holding in his hand the key to the bottomless pit and a great chain. And he seized the dragon, that ancient serpent, who is the devil and Satan, and bound him for a thousand years.

The thousand years referenced here is symbolic of the entire church age, and therefore it makes good sense to see this passage as parallel to Jesus's words about binding the strong man. In other words, Jesus is not casting out demons by the power of the Devil. He is casting out demons because he has overpowered the Devil.

"Wake up and see what I am doing!" he cries. "I am conquering!"

"No servant can serve two masters."

"Whoever is not with me is against me."

"Whoever loves father or mother more than me is not worthy of me, and whoever loves son or daughter more than me is not worthy of me."

Why? Because none of them holds your eternal salvation in his or her hand as Christ does. Because he conquers sin, vanquishes Satan and his demons, swallows up death, heals and forgives, and secures for all eternity. Because all of the stuff is his.

The world stands opposed, nonchalant, blasé about Christ. But none of them have bound the strong man.

Victory is coming. So what will our response be? Which side will we be on?

> "Truly, I say to you, all sins will be forgiven the children of man, and whatever blasphemies they utter, but whoever blasphemes against the Holy Spirit never has forgiveness, but is guilty of an eternal sin"—for they were saying, "He has an unclean spirit." (Mark 3:28–30)

All sins and blasphemies will be forgiven of every repentant person. What a gracious God we serve!

But this "blasphemy against the Holy Spirit." What is that?

The blasphemy against the Holy Spirit is an eternal sin with a gravity to it that sets it apart from every other sin. It is not especially clear that Jesus is saying the scribes have already committed this unpardonable sin, but he *is* certainly warning them about it. In some sense, he is saying, "You fellows are on a very dangerous track." By attributing the work of Christ to the work of Satan, they are committing the unpardonable sin of eternally rejecting Jesus.

I believe the unforgivable sin is this: enduringly unrepentant resistance to Jesus. We know that to reject Jesus is to accept condemnation: "Whoever believes in the Son has eternal life; whoever does not obey the Son shall not see life, but the wrath of God remains on him" (John 3:36).

Because it is the Holy Spirit's job to glorify Jesus, to permanently reject Jesus is to blaspheme the Spirit. To ultimately place your allegiance against Christ—and remember, not to align with him is to essentially align against him—will not be forgiven. This statement, if anything, contradicts all sentimental notions of universalism or inclusivism. To stand against Christ with finality is to fall on the final day.

This is why, when you hear the good report of Christ's victory over sin and death, it behooves you not to harden your heart but to lay hold in faith of the kingdom.

On the flip side, if the only unpardonable sin is enduring unrepentance, this means repentance receives the pardon of "all sins and whatever blasphemies." Oh, if we could only truly see how much we've been set free from! The spoils of salvation victory are superabundant—all because Jesus is Lord of all and was, is, and will be forever victorious. His earthly ministry has thrown a wrench into the mechanism of history—we call that wrench *the cross*—and now the gears are turning the other way. What do these miracles of deliverance from demons—not to mention his command of nature and his healing of diseases—reveal except that he is reversing the curse?

At the cross, Jesus accomplishes the beautiful, scandalous irony of turning his apparent defeat into his decisive victory over his enemies. At the cross, "He disarmed the rulers and authorities and put them to open shame, by triumphing over them in him" (Col. 2:15). He crushes the head of the Serpent with his heel. And then! In his resurrection, Christ emerges the ruler of the grave. Death swallows him up like the whale did Jonah, but Jesus poisons death's guts, eating it from the inside out, until death cannot help but spit him out three days later. And now he casts out the forces of wickedness, not by the force of wickedness but by the force of his hell-proof, sin-proof, death-proof nature. The risen Christ is the invincible God.

You want to make sure this very moment that you are on the right side of victory.

We close with this stirring reflection from David Powlison:

> Jesus Christ is the triumphant Deliverer and King. Jesus, the pioneer and perfecter of faith, the Lord of glory, brings light and life. He is the man over whom Satan could gain no control. The Son of God loved his Father with no sinful remainder or qualifier, and he lives.
>
> The life, death, resurrection, and ascension of Jesus Christ reversed the tide of war. The King appeared, single-handedly

breaking the stranglehold of the oppressor. Christians believe Jesus' words that his death and resurrection will cast out the devil. . . . Jesus speaks of his cross as the definitive cosmic exorcism. This event—the only exorcism in the gospel of John—breaks Satan's hold over the world. . . . We experience deliverance from the power of Satan when we turn consciously from darkness to the light. The one who blinds us that we might wallow in lies, lusts, and misery is sentenced to everlasting darkness, while we who once lived in fear of death now rise to life in hope of the resurrection. Through the Holy Spirit, we are in Christ and Christ is in us. As freed captives we are learning to love our King and are unlearning the ways of our former oppressor and master. Death and sin no longer have the last say.[2]

---

[2] David Powlison, *Power Encounters: Reclaiming Spiritual Warfare* (Grand Rapids, MI: Baker, 1995), 21–22.

# 8

# Weeping and Waking

Jesus had friends. It might seem strange to think about this aspect of Jesus's life. He had disciples, certainly, and they were his friends, but then there was that circle within the circle—Peter, James, and John. And John is singled out still further as "the disciple whom Jesus loved" (John 21:20). In addition to these fellows, it appears from the Gospels that Jesus had honest-to-goodness friendships, as you or I might—people he considered closer than others, people with whom he felt a kinship beyond the ordinary, people with whom he shared that special, unquantifiable "Me, too!" kind of chemistry.

It is difficult thinking about what life might have been like following Jesus during his earthly ministry. But can you imagine what it might have been like to be one of his friends? You would have gotten to know what made Jesus laugh, what he liked to eat, how he liked to spend his (very minimal) free time. You could have heard his ruminations in his most private moments, the ones not recorded for all posterity in the Scriptures. You could have come closest to the verity of his humanity and seen, even in his off minutes, when Jesus kicked his feet up or let his guard down, the verity of his deity.

I am certain that Jesus was the best friend anyone could ever have, but I also cannot help but think that those closest to Jesus must have constantly dealt with placing unreasonable expectations on him. Certainly as a sinless man and as very God, Jesus was capable of a great many extraordinary things, of anything good really. But as we see with the disciples, I expect that Jesus's friends were often tempted to want to use him. They probably desired special treatment and certainly they harbored special hopes.

I think we see in the story of the death of Lazarus what kind of disappointment results from having expectations of friendship with Jesus. Martha and Mary both know that Jesus could have saved their brother Lazarus from dying. They both say as much. What they reveal is human, natural, logical. In the depths of their grief, they are wrestling with what they know Jesus can do and, therefore, in their estimation, what he *should have* done. But being friends with Jesus is not quite so simple as getting whatever you ask.

Many times we expect Jesus to provide certain things for us or to answer our prayers in certain ways, all along without understanding that the plans he has for us are actually far better than what we're demanding of him.

## The Death That Is Not Death

What is death but the supreme evidence that the world is broken? I have preached numerous funerals throughout my ministry, many of them for departed unbelievers of largely unbelieving families. These services are always difficult in a variety of ways, but the one point I make in my funeral homily that nearly everyone agrees with—especially in times of grief—is that death is not the way things are supposed to be. Even the person who, in the normal course of living, sentimentally believes death is merely a "return to the earth" in the cycle of life can feel in the depths of mourning that death is tragic, hurtful, and wrong in some way.

Death tells us that the world is broken. And when we follow that conclusion back to its foundations, we are faced with the more difficult truth that the world is broken because sin has corrupted the goodness of creation and its creatures.

When I am preaching a funeral service, I remind those in attendance that the moment we are sharing is real life. We see death as an interruption, but this is only because we spend so much time not thinking about our mortality, or trying not to. But death gets our attention. It heightens our sense of earthly living. Funerals are irruptions of the real. A funeral is Romans 8:23 with a suit on.

In response to this, we want to prolong life. That is our expectation—to make life better, more comfortable, easier, and above all, longer. Advances in medicine are helping us do just that. When a young person dies, we are prone to say, "He was taken before his time." And the goal for all of us is to make sure "our time" is as put off as we can manage it.

Prolonging life is an admirable goal in a lot of ways. But it is certainly not integral to Jesus's message. The way of Christ, instead, is always to blow our expectations out of the water. He may interrupt our comfortable lives with suffering, but his solution for suffering is far above what we can dream or imagine.

> Now a certain man was ill, Lazarus of Bethany, the village of Mary and her sister Martha. It was Mary who anointed the Lord with ointment and wiped his feet with her hair, whose brother Lazarus was ill. So the sisters sent to him, saying, "Lord, he whom you love is ill." But when Jesus heard it he said, "This illness does not lead to death. It is for the glory of God, so that the Son of God may be glorified through it."
>
> Now Jesus loved Martha and her sister and Lazarus. So, when he heard that Lazarus was ill, he stayed two days longer in the place where he was. (John 11:1–6)

The expectation of the sisters is that Jesus will hurry to Lazarus's side and deliver him from his illness. They do not doubt he is perfectly able to do such a thing. The implication is that the illness is quite serious, thus the need to summon Jesus.

The Lord's response, then, is quite curious: "This illness does not lead to death" (v. 4). He cannot mean that the illness will not be fatal, because verse 6 implies he tarries precisely so that Lazarus will die. (This despite v. 12 informing us the disciples understand Jesus to mean the illness will not be fatal.) So what can Jesus mean by saying that the illness will not lead to death? D. A. Carson explains that he means "it will not *end*—ultimately—in death."[1]

No, Lazarus will in fact die. It is the Lord's will to ensure it. But it is not the Lord's will that death have the last word. He plans, in some mysterious way, to leverage the death of Lazarus for his own glory. There is a miracle in the works that will reveal the glory of Christ in a way unlike any other.

And because the glory of Christ so outshines everything, even death itself must be reconsidered. This is why Jesus insists on referring to the departed as "sleeping." Death loses its finality in the hands of the alpha and omega. Death is not death for those safely held in the arms of Jesus.

## That We May Die with Him

C. S. Lewis writes: "Die before you die. There is no chance after."[2]

In Luke 13:1–5, Jesus is asked about the horrific incident of Pilate mixing the blood of murdered Galileans with their sacrifices. Jesus responds with a very specific theological point meant to broaden our understanding of death's reach and purpose. As in the fatal fall of the tower at Siloam, he says, everyone will die. Your categories of good and bad matter not one whit. Sinners and saints alike will suffer. In this sense, death is senseless. It behooves you, then, according to Jesus, to repent and believe. You don't know when death will claim you, and you want to be spiritually prepared when it does. You cannot avoid death. But you can avoid the death *after* death. Provided, of course, you are willing to die not just for Jesus but *in* Jesus.

> Then after this he said to the disciples, "Let us go to Judea again." The disciples said to him, "Rabbi, the Jews were just now seeking to stone you, and are you going there again?"

---

[1] D. A. Carson, *The Gospel according to John* (Grand Rapids, MI: Eerdmans, 1991), 406. Emphasis original.
[2] C. S. Lewis, *Till We Have Faces: A Myth Retold* (London: Collins, 1980), 291.

Jesus answered, "Are there not twelve hours in the day? If anyone walks in the day, he does not stumble, because he sees the light of this world. But if anyone walks in the night, he stumbles, because the light is not in him." After saying these things, he said to them, "Our friend Lazarus has fallen asleep, but I go to awaken him." The disciples said to him, "Lord, if he has fallen asleep, he will recover." Now Jesus had spoken of his death, but they thought that he meant taking rest in sleep. Then Jesus told them plainly, "Lazarus has died, and for your sake I am glad that I was not there, so that you may believe. But let us go to him." So Thomas, called the Twin, said to his fellow disciples, "Let us also go, that we may die with him." (John 11:7–16)

Thomas doesn't even know what he's talking about, but his courage and loyalty are true. His cry then becomes the forerunner of Revelation 12:11: "And they have conquered him by the blood of the Lamb and by the word of their testimony, for they loved not their lives even unto death."

It is dangerous, apparently, for Jesus to travel to Judea. His intentional delay, in fact, may serve a dual purpose. It ensures Lazarus will pass, of course, but it also gives ample warning to Jesus's enemies that he may be traveling to the area. These enemies are not to be trifled with. Lazarus's death, then, brings up the specter of martyrdom for Jesus and his disciples. But Thomas, at least, is willing to brave the danger.

He is not emboldened, as one might suppose, by Jesus's promise to "awaken" Lazarus, as if understanding the implications of Christ's resurrection power. No, he is simply emboldened by his love for Jesus. If Jesus goes to be stoned, Thomas reasons, let his followers go and be stoned alongside him.

But his statement is truer than he knows. Knowing what *we* know about Jesus's resurrection power, we can say, "Let us also go, that we may die with him." Paul writes in Romans 6:8, "Now if we have died with Christ, we believe that we will also live with him."

You aren't promised tomorrow or even your next breath. I may not get through writing this page. You may not get through reading it. It is imperative that before you die, you die with Christ. It is the only way to conquer death.

## The Son of God, Who Is Coming into the World

It seems likely that even if Jesus does not delay, Lazarus will die before he arrives. The journey Jesus has to take to Bethany is estimated by some as a two-day walk. But in the delay, Jesus ensures that enough days pass for Lazarus to be dead long enough to ward off any rumors of resuscitations and the like. John 11:17 reads, "Now when Jesus came, he found that Lazarus had already been in the tomb four days." This amount of time is sufficient to demonstrate that Lazarus is indeed dead, that he was in need of all the burial preparations, and that the decay of his body has already begun.

Thus, the scene Jesus and his disciples arrive to is one of full-on mourning:

> Bethany was near Jerusalem, about two miles off, and many of the Jews had come to Martha and Mary to console them concerning their brother. So when Martha heard that Jesus was coming, she went and met him, but Mary remained seated in the house. Martha said to Jesus, "Lord, if you had been here, my brother would not have died. But even now I know that whatever you ask from God, God will give you." Jesus said to her, "Your brother will rise again." Martha said to him, "I know that he will rise again in the resurrection on the last day." Jesus said to her, "I am the resurrection and the life. Whoever believes in me, though he die, yet shall he live, and everyone who lives and believes in me shall never die. Do you believe this?" She said to him, "Yes, Lord; I believe that you are the Christ, the Son of God, who is coming into the world." (John 11:18–27)

The question Jesus asks Martha is another of those God-authored inquiries designed to lay a heart bare and expose its true colors. From the beginning, God asks his people questions for which he already knows the answers but with which he plans to elicit deep meaning. The first is "Where are you?" (Gen. 3:9), followed shortly thereafter by "Who told you that you were naked? Have you eaten of the tree of which I commanded you not to eat?" (v. 11). Of Cain, God asks, "Where is Abel your brother?" (4:9).

Did God not know the answers to these questions? Of course he did.

Jesus is fantastically good at asking such questions. This exchange with the scribes is a great example:

> And they came again to Jerusalem. And as he was walking in the temple, the chief priests and the scribes and the elders came to him, and they said to him, "By what authority are you doing these things, or who gave you this authority to do them?" Jesus said to them, "I will ask you one question; answer me, and I will tell you by what authority I do these things. Was the baptism of John from heaven or from man? Answer me." And they discussed it with one another, saying, "If we say, 'From heaven,' he will say, 'Why then did you not believe him?' But shall we say, 'From man'?"—they were afraid of the people, for they all held that John really was a prophet. So they answered Jesus, "We do not know." And Jesus said to them, "Neither will I tell you by what authority I do these things." (Mark 11:27–33)

Jesus knows what they believe. He just wants to see if they'll be honest about it. His question ingeniously reveals their hollow authority. They try to corner the most towering intellect in the history of the universe, and he pulls the ol' switcheroo on 'em. He asks the scribes a question designed to either show their colors or shut them up, and they come back with a dishonest answer. And when you try to tell lies to Jesus, he won't have it.

The most penetrating question Jesus ever asks, however, is probably "Who do you say that I am?" (Matt. 16:15). Cutting through the cultural buzz, the word on the street, the popular perceptions and misperceptions about himself, Jesus asks Peter directly, "Who am I?" This is essentially what he does for the grieving Martha.

"Martha," he reasons, "put your grief in context. Are you one who will grieve as those who have no hope? Or will you grieve your loss as if the ultimate consoler of grief—indeed, as if the very reverser of death—were right here holding your hand?"

No one who believes in Jesus will die. *Do you believe this?*

Like Peter's, Martha's confession is rock-solid, one for the endless ages: "Yes, Lord; I believe that you are the Christ, the Son of God, who is coming into the world" (John 11:27).

Certainly this puts death in a different light, doesn't it? It puts death in the light of the radiance of God's glory, in fact; the light that drives out the darkness of death.

God's plan for the world, after all, is not to let the rebellion of his creatures set the course. He made this place good and he made us good, so he will not stand for the triumph of death. No, in fact, he will stand upon the earth in the last day (Job 19:25), having risen as the sun with healing in his wings (Mal. 4:2), a testimony to the unfailing life he ontologically and eternally is, and while death may take our mortality, we will, even in tangible flesh, with material yet incorruptible eyeballs, behold him (Job 19:26).

God's vision for his world is not for death's victory but his own. His vision is for the entire earth to be covered with the knowledge of his glory like the waters cover the sea (Hab. 2:14). The knowledge of his glory climaxes in Christ, the very revelation of his glory (Heb. 1:3), and so it is no wonder that Christ is called the lamp of the new heaven and the new earth (Rev. 21:23). How better could God flood the earth with his glory than by filling it with the endless beatific rays of the Son?

When Thomas says, "Let us also go, that we may die with him," he speaks the unwitting truth. When Martha says, "You are the Christ, the Son of God, who is coming into the world," she speaks the unwitting truth.

In the Gospels, we are viewing the kingdom of God coming into the world through the works and words of his Son, Jesus Christ, and he is steadily and certainly filling all things (Eph. 4:10). He fills even the grave with life.

## The Affectionate Christ

One aspect of Christ's glory we see in the story of the raising of Lazarus puts skin, hair, and tears on the incarnation.

> When she had said this, she went and called her sister Mary, saying in private, "The Teacher is here and is calling for you." And when she heard it, she rose quickly and went to him. Now Jesus had not yet come into the village, but was still in the place where Martha had met him. When the Jews who were with her in the house, consoling her, saw Mary rise quickly and go out, they followed her, supposing that she was going to the tomb to weep there. Now when Mary came to where Jesus was and saw him, she fell at his feet, saying to him, "Lord, if you had been here, my brother would not have died." When Jesus saw her weeping, and the Jews who had come with her also weeping, he was deeply moved in his spirit and greatly troubled. And he said, "Where have you laid him?" They said to him, "Lord, come and see." Jesus wept. So the Jews said, "See how he loved him!" But some of them said, "Could not he who opened the eyes of the blind man also have kept this man from dying?" (John 11:28–37)

Mary's statement to Jesus in verse 32 carries an aggrieved sense of injustice: this should not have happened. You should have done something. This isn't right.

Mary's objection is essential to human nature, fractured by sin but still in the *imago Dei*, haunted by natural law, by the residue of moral absolutism.

Your anger about death is evidence of God's existence. You can't get moral outrage, a sense of evil, from naturalism and moral relativism. If we are just the random accumulation of billions of years of the happenstantial progress of natural processes, we have no justification for saying death is wrong, much less that murders of the innocent, genocide, or what have you is wrong. Naturalism and its evolutionary philosophies consequently don't teach protection of the weakest and most vulnerable, but instead survival of the fittest.

But atheists and other secular humanists today say they *can* be moral, that morality evolves as we do and as society progresses. But what they mean by morality is simply utilitarianism—what is moral is whatever is beneficial to the species as a whole at the given time. So they say it was wrong for Adam Lanza to murder twenty-seven people, including little children, at Sandy Hook Elementary School in Newtown, Connecticut, because what benefits society at this stage of our progress is protection of the weak. Or, more precisely, it was wrong to murder twenty-seven people because their families wanted them to remain alive (which is why atheists think nothing of the roughly three thousand murders occurring every day under the label "abortion").

But can this sort of utilitarian logic speak to our innate sense of outrage? Murder is wrong because it isn't beneficial at a given time? It is wrong based on the evolved values of our society? These rationales cannot say that what happened in Newtown on December 14, 2012, will be wrong in one hundred years, much less that the slaughter of the Canaanites was wrong four thousand years ago.

But the Christian says, "No, murder is wrong, because it is wrong." It is wrong because God says, "Thou shalt not kill" (Ex. 20:13, KJV), because he has created man and woman in his image, and therefore life is precious, all human life, whether it's useful to you or not, beneficial to society or not, full of promise or not. The killing of innocent children is evil precisely because we have a holy God who declares what is good and what is evil. And the reason you know instinctively there are some things that are good and some things that are wrong is not because of the proper firings of synapses in your brain or the sentimental attachments you've developed over time, but because God has put inside of you a sense of justice.

It is this sense of justice violated that drives Mary's expectations, and it is the full weight of justice—that there must be death because sin has merited it and that the Christ must be crucified because God's glory demands it—that drives Jesus's reaction.

Verses 33–35 reveal an extraordinary glimpse into Jesus's humanity. In verse 33, Jesus's reaction to Mary's inconsolable grief—more emotion-laden than Martha's, it would seem—is apparently shaded in most English translations. Stephen Evans points out that the Greek text "literally implies that Jesus 'snorted within himself,' like a horse."[3]

Jesus's inward trouble, then, is frustration or exasperation over the inherent disbelief in his power over death. If he has the power to cure a deadly illness, one might reason, couldn't he have the power to cure death itself? Their doubt is evident (v. 37).

But grief is its own logic. And Jesus understands that. So he is not just disappointed in his friends' lack of faith; he is disappointed along with them about death itself. The shortest verse in the Bible reads, "Jesus wept" (v. 35). Separated as they are by the directions to Lazarus's grave (v. 34), it is not likely that Jesus's weeping is for the same reason as his harrumphing. As most interpreters agree, Jesus is weeping because his friend Lazarus has died.

More deeply than that, however, Jesus is weeping because death is real. He has utter confidence in the Father that his sovereignty is being made manifest, even over death. He knows what the disciples and his friends don't yet grasp—that death is to be conquered and vanquished. But he also knows the price that must be paid to secure the will of the Father in relation to this death. And he knows the sheer offense against God's holiness that has made death necessary. It is an offense against himself, as well.

So even though Jesus is about to bring life to Lazarus, and even though he knows he will himself conquer the grave, he is moved to tears because death is serious business.

What a comfort to know that not only is God not ambivalent about death, he is not unfamiliar with it! Jesus knows what it's like

---

[3] C. Stephen Evans, *The Historical Christ and the Jesus of Faith: The Incarnational Narrative as History* (Oxford: Oxford University Press, 1996), 341.

to grieve. He knows what it's like to hurt. He knows what it's like to feel abandoned (Matt. 27:46; Ps. 22:1).

All of this is bound up in the emotional response of Jesus to the entire situation. He is not some passive observer of the foibles of mankind. He is an active participant. God has not kept his distance but has put skin on. He has gotten his hands dirty. And now he uses them to wipe away tears and to usher us into the glory of the affectionate Savior.

Again, Evans writes:

> The story then is not just about Lazarus but about the intense relationship between Jesus and two women friends. It is a relationship that is put under severe strain, but one in which the mutual love and loyalty between Jesus, Mary, and Martha finally triumph, as seen in Jesus' miracle on the one hand, and the anointing of Jesus by Mary that follows in chapter 12 on the other.[4]

Mary's tears of grief become the oil of gladness. This is the fullness of the aim of the incarnation. God defies expectations of him by becoming man. And the God-man defies expectations of him by skipping a healing to go straight to a resurrection. Thus, he shows the true depths of his affection for his friends.

## The Resurrection and the Life

Paul tells the timid Timothy, "God gave us a spirit not of fear" (2 Tim. 1:7). Therefore, the command echoes down through eternity: "Be not afraid."

Why? Because death can be avoided? No, because we know that greater is he that is in us than he that is in the world (1 John 4:4). Greater is he who is life itself than he whose weapon is death.

We weep with those who weep, we bring comfort to those who mourn, but we take courage because we know that sin and death are not the end of the story. We know that death's days are num-

---

[4] Ibid., 342.

bered. We know that those who mourn may be comforted because Christ has triumphed over sin at the cross and has triumphed over death in his resurrection, and so he has given his word that he will have the final word:

> Then I saw a new heaven and a new earth, for the first heaven and the first earth had passed away, and the sea was no more. And I saw the holy city, new Jerusalem, coming down out of heaven from God, prepared as a bride adorned for her husband. And I heard a loud voice from the throne saying, "Behold, the dwelling place of God is with man. He will dwell with them, and they will be his people, and God himself will be with them as their God. He will wipe away every tear from their eyes, and death shall be no more, neither shall there be mourning, nor crying, nor pain anymore, for the former things have passed away."
>
> And he who was seated on the throne said, "Behold, I am making all things new." Also he said, "Write this down, for these words are trustworthy and true." (Rev. 21:1–5)

Because God and his Word are trustworthy and true, we don't have to attend the agendas of the world that is grasping at straws right now to find a sliver of comfort and explanation for the death we realize is not the way it is supposed to be. We don't have to be constantly apologizing for our faith, either, and coddling doubt and putting out apologetic fires. We know the future; we have the thirty-thousand-foot view. We know the end.

And this is great cause for optimism, for hope. We cannot grieve as those who have no hope, because Jesus is making all things new. There is a day of no death, no sorrow, and no pain. He has promised it and he will deliver it.

> Then Jesus, deeply moved again, came to the tomb. It was a cave, and a stone lay against it. Jesus said, "Take away the stone." Martha, the sister of the dead man, said to him, "Lord, by this time there will be an odor, for he has been dead four

days." Jesus said to her, "Did I not tell you that if you believed you would see the glory of God?" So they took away the stone. And Jesus lifted up his eyes and said, "Father, I thank you that you have heard me. I knew that you always hear me, but I said this on account of the people standing around, that they may believe that you sent me." When he had said these things, he cried out with a loud voice, "Lazarus, come out." The man who had died came out, his hands and feet bound with linen strips, and his face wrapped with a cloth. Jesus said to them, "Unbind him, and let him go." (John 11:38–44)

One thing I always point out about this passage when teaching it is that Lazarus does not need seven steps or tips about how to achieve a successful exit from the tomb. No, he simply needs the word of Christ. He is raised by command. Jesus gives the word and Lazarus is made alive. He cannot help but obey.

In the same way, when God raises our dead hearts, they are truly raised. And when Christ commands us to come forth from the tombs of spiritual death, he is staking his claim on us. We belong to him. He has brought us into the land of the living, removing our burial clothes and replacing them with the cloaks of his righteousness. Of the Christian man he commands life, and of sin and death he commands, "Unbind him, and let him go." We are no longer enslaved to death.

Not even are we enslaved—oh, this is amazing!—to *physical* death. Even if we die, we don't die.

We will weep no more, and waking will be all there is.

# 9

# Get-Up Time

Christianity, according to C. S. Lewis, "is the story of how the rightful king has landed, you might say landed in disguise, and is calling us all to take part in a great campaign of sabotage."[1] In the Gospels, sermon by sermon, story by story, miracle by miracle, Jesus is heralding and actualizing the blessing of his saving sovereignty. He shows us what he calls us into, that we might be inexorably drawn by the power of the Spirit working through the revelation of his glory into his light and life, that is, into the kingdom. Even now, the glorious light of Jesus Christ is flooding into history and establishing the bright beacon of the hope to be found in the kingdom of God.

When the prisoners of sin and death were freed during Jesus's earthly campaign, the result was incomparable joy. The gospel's recruits exulted like never before:

- When they saw the star, they rejoiced exceedingly with great joy (Matt. 2:10).
- [T]hey were all amazed and glorified God, saying, "We never saw anything like this!" (Mark 2:12).
- And amazement seized them all, and they glorified God and were filled with awe, saying, "We have seen extraordinary things today" (Luke 5:26).
- And the men marveled, saying, "What sort of man is this, that even winds and sea obey him?" (Matt. 8:27).

---

[1] C. S. Lewis, *Mere Christianity* (New York: HarperCollins, 2001), 46.

- They said to each other, "Did not our hearts burn within us while he talked to us on the road, while he opened to us the Scriptures?" (Luke 24:32).
- So they departed quickly from the tomb with fear and great joy, and ran to tell his disciples (Matt. 28:8).

These are the cries of those who are passing from death to life. And the exultation continues today for those who grasp the depths of their despair and have been laid hold of by the strong arm of the Savior. The joy is so great, so abounding, so all-encompassing and ever-flowing that it refashions hopes and dreams, and sends fears and worries scurrying away.

The church I pastor, Middletown Springs Community Church in Vermont, sits on a quintessential New England town green, and kitty-corner from us is the old town cemetery (maintained to impeccable vision by one of our church members). Many of the graves in the Middletown cemetery date to before the Declaration of Independence. Some of the tombstones are unreadable due to age and weather. But some of these historical markers are legible still, and they hark back to a time when people knew what to put on a headstone. Here is just one of my favorite epitaphs:

Death my friends is nothing frightful
  If we're prepared to go.
Jesus makes all things delightful
  When we leave this world of woe.

Now here, in four lines of simple verse, is a theology of the kingdom! Christ indeed turns mourning into laughter, fear into confidence, even death to life. The curse in Christ is immanently reversible. And that is beyond delightful.

## Of Dads and Daughters

The first deep acquaintance with grief for my wife and me came upon the miscarriage of our second baby. We had both lost loved ones before, but until then we had never been so personally affected, Becky especially.

I remember the first signs that something was wrong, causes enough to head to the doctor for answers. I remember most vividly sitting in a dim ultrasound room while the technician ran the probe over my wife's belly. The technician had an assistant with her, and they talked in very hushed tones. They said nothing to us that I recall. They discussed what they were seeing—and what they weren't seeing. They were keeping us in the dark until the doctor could speak to us, and that is exactly how we felt—as if a darkness was overcoming us.

Later, the doctor confirmed that we had lost our child. The shock was profound. I could not think, could not feel. I remember, as Becky and I sat in the examination room still reeling from the news, both of us numb to the bones but feeling a thousand pounds heavy, some idiotic male nurse coming into the room and making a joke, and then, when neither of us responded, making another joke about us being a "tough crowd" or some such thing. I want to think now that he did not know what news we'd just received; otherwise, surely he would not have so stupidly tried to cheer us up. Or perhaps he had not been well trained in bedside manner. In any event, what he did was extremely callous. If I'd had the energy, I would have really let him have it. Instead, I seethed. I felt as if death itself was mocking us.

Becky's shock lasted several days. The outpouring of emotions came later, as the process of grief passed. I was broken by the next day myself and spent most of that day sobbing uncontrollably into our bed. We decided to name our baby Angel, and as the grief subsided, we embraced the certain hope that we will be reunited with Angel in heaven.

A few months later, we were pregnant again. This pregnancy was difficult. Stress and other factors complicated our baby's growth and caused Becky lots of discomfort and anxiety. After the miscarriage of Angel, we were pretty scared about how things might turn out with this new pregnancy.

Our second daughter was carried all the way to term. I remember her birth, however, and while she came much more quickly than our first child, there was a complication. The doctor was concerned about her position, about the position of the umbilical cord. When our baby was delivered, she did not cry. The silence was unnerving.

I remember the nurse bringing our little baby over to the bassinet. The nurse looked concerned. I had been videotaping the event, but I put the camera down. I could tell something was wrong. Our baby was having trouble breathing. The more frantic the nurse looked, the more frightened I got. After multiple attempts to clear her throat and lungs, finally, climactically, our daughter let out the most beautiful wail I've ever heard.

We named her Grace. She was born on July 5, a year after the passing of our little Angel. Joyfully, wonderfully, ecstatically, Grace has not shut up since.

Jesus makes all things new.

I carry all of that stress, fear, wonder, and joy into Mark's account of Jesus and Jairus's daughter.

> And when Jesus had crossed again in the boat to the other side, a great crowd gathered about him, and he was beside the sea. Then came one of the rulers of the synagogue, Jairus by name, and seeing him, he fell at his feet and implored him earnestly, saying, "My little daughter is at the point of death. Come and lay your hands on her, so that she may be made well and live." (Mark 5:21–23)

Just previous, the Gerasene demoniac falls at Jesus's feet, too (v. 6). Falling at Jesus's feet is an essential part of faith.

In contrast, however, the herdsmen who witness Jesus's power in the exorcism of the Gerasene basically say, "Go away" (v. 17), while one of the rulers of the synagogue says, "Please come." This certainly puts a new spin on the notion that working-class Joes take to Jesus like a baby to candy while the religious leaders bristle at his every word. What makes the difference in this instance?

Well, in the case of the herdsmen, Jesus has just caused the destruction of two thousand pieces of their property (v. 13). Jairus stands to lose a lot in his fraternization with Jesus in terms of his position and reputation, but he has counted the cost, and he can see that he is on the verge of losing something much more precious: "my little daughter."

Later we learn that she's twelve. She is not so little anymore, but we who are dads of daughters know that no matter how old they get, they are always our little girls.

The term of endearment shows the dad's deep affection, and Jesus echoes it later, echoing the affection with a resonance deeper than even the child's biological father could manage.

Still, the combination of Jairus's fear and faith makes for a powerful request: "Come and lay your hands on her, so that she may be made well and live."

This is what I prayed in the darkness of that ultrasound room. This is what I prayed at Gracie's side while she gasped for her first breaths. This is, in a way, what I prayed for Becky and for myself in the midst of our grief and fear: "We need your touch, Jesus. We feel death. Please put your hands on us and make it go away."

When you ask Jesus in faith to come, he always says yes:

And he went with him.
    And a great crowd followed him and thronged about him.
(v. 24)

At this point, the narrative is interrupted by another encounter, Jesus's healing of the woman with a bloody discharge. This is not a Markan arrangement for effect—the entire incident is recorded as unfolding the same way in Matthew and Luke—but a divine orchestration. The healing of the woman reveals its own lessons (as covered in chapter 5), but in its providential diversion, it serves much the same as Jesus's delay in coming to Lazarus. In short, the encounter with the woman gives Jairus's daughter time to die:

While he was still speaking [to the woman he had healed of a bloody discharge], there came from the ruler's house some

who said, "Your daughter is dead. Why trouble the Teacher
any further?" (v. 35)

Do you feel that? It is despair. It is profound disappointment.
It may, in fact, be the onset of anger.

Sometimes it seems Jesus takes much too long. I know he's
never early, but it often seems as if he's late—too late, even.

I wonder what Jairus is thinking throughout Jesus's exchange
with the woman. He issues no objections that we are aware of, but
surely his anxiety begins to creep up. Like Martha and Mary, he
has expressed faith in Jesus's healing power. But perhaps he is not
yet confident in or even aware of Jesus's resurrecting power.

Jesus drives out the rumbles of worry:

> But overhearing what they said, Jesus said to the ruler of
> the synagogue, "Do not fear, only believe." And he allowed
> no one to follow him except Peter and James and John the
> brother of James. They came to the house of the ruler of the
> synagogue, and Jesus saw a commotion, people weeping and
> wailing loudly. (vv. 36–38)

The girl's fate is already deemed sealed; thus, as Matthew 9:23
shows, the professional mourners have already shown up. But Jesus
likes showing up when it seems he is too late. Hope shines brightest
when it seems all hope is gone:

> And when he had entered, he said to them, "Why are you
> making a commotion and weeping? The child is not dead but
> sleeping." (Mark 5:39)

For the faithful, the miracle-pregnant words of Jesus in the midst
of grief are great comfort. For the worldly, they are foolishness.

> And they laughed at him. But he put them all outside and
> took the child's father and mother and those who were with
> him and went in where the child was. (v. 40)

In my retrospective fantasies, Jesus comes into that somber examination room on July 3, 2002, takes that moron nurse by the arm, and "puts him outside."

There will come a day when those who mock the faithful, who jeer at them for both their grief and their hope, will get their comeuppance. If it seems to take too long, do not doubt its coming. The church will not suffer the derision of the world one second longer than God has planned. In a splendid vision of exulting triumph, the Lord will put the jawing and the sneering away. And he will take his children by the hand and deliver them:

> Taking her by the hand he said to her, "Talitha cumi," which means, "Little girl, I say to you, arise." (v. 41)

*Talitha* literally means "little girl." With this term of endearment, Jesus shares the affection of the girl's father. In the parlance of that day, however, the word *talitha* would be more akin to our "sweetie" or "honey." *Cumi*, on the other hand, basically means "get up." Do you see what Jesus is doing here? The girl has died, but because he is Jesus the Lord, God in the flesh, sovereign over life and death, the head of all rule and authority, the alpha and the omega, the first and the last, the sustainer of the universe by a mere word from his lips, he is treating her like it's time to eat breakfast and get ready for school: "Sweetie, it's time to get up."

Of this account, Tim Keller writes in *King's Cross*:

> Jesus is doing exactly what this child's parents might do on a sunny morning. He sits down, takes her hand, and says, "Honey, it's time to get up." And she does. Jesus is facing the most implacable, inexorable enemy of the human race and such is his power that he holds this child by the hand and gently lifts her right up through it. "Honey, get up." Jesus is saying by his actions, "If I have you by the hand, death itself is nothing but sleep."
>
> There's nothing more frightening for a little child than to lose the hand of the parent in a crowd or in the dark, but

that is nothing compared with Jesus's own loss. He lost his Father's hand on the cross. He went into the tomb so we can be raised out of it. He lost hold of his Father's hand so we could know that once he has us by the hand, he will never, ever forsake us.[2]

All of the grief, all of the pain, all of the fear, all of the weight of the entire broken mess of life is brought down to the finest point of a hush in the gentle words, "It's time to get up, Honey." Just as he made the wild storm immediately calm at his command, Jesus instantaneously makes death stop.

I cannot wait to meet Angel. I cannot wait to see her smile. I presume she was a daughter. God has given me two beautiful growing daughters. They are light and joy in my life. He wanted me to have daughters. So I picture Angel's smile like her mother's, sparkling blue eyes like her mother's, a gentle wisp of a hand. And perhaps Christ will grant this fantasy: that when my life on this earth is no more, I will wake to the wonder of his glorious might and all-consuming presence with Angel at my side, holding my hand, and saying sweetly in the heavenly tongue, "Time to get up, Daddy."

## That Consummate Morn

What Paul describes in 1 Corinthians 15 beggars belief. It seems too good to be true. We will explore its truth in the next chapter, but as the fulfillment of what is foreshadowed in Mark 5, it gives the glow of glory to Jairus's daughter.

Of course, all of the resurrections in the Gospels, save Jesus's own, are not resurrections as we should hope for. They are miracles of the most astounding quality indeed, but even they pale compared to the glory to be revealed. Lazarus had to die again. The widow from Nain's son had to die again. Jairus's daughter had to die again.

---

[2] Timothy Keller, *King's Cross: The Story of the World in the Life of Jesus* (New York: Dutton, 2011), 68–69.

There is a better resurrection to come.

I suppose Jairus's wish is that she will outlive her old man. Maybe she does. But in either event, perhaps his vision of death is totally changed. It should be, anyway! He should see death in an entirely new light after this:

> And immediately the girl got up and began walking (for she was twelve years of age), and they were immediately overcome with amazement. (Mark 5:42)

I should say so! Being overcome with amazement is exactly the sort of reaction due the power of Christ. After the raising of the widow's son, the cry goes up, "God has visited his people!" (Luke 7:16).

That is exactly what resurrection is. If death is the price for sin (Rom. 6:23), and sin is falling short of God's glory (Rom. 3:23), it only makes sense that when God's glory comes near, death is replaced by life (Rom. 6:4).

Every resurrection in the Scriptures is a picture of that moment, the final keeping of the promise of conversion, sanctification, and glorification: the future resurrection, when we are not raised in our perishable bodies but raised *changed*, incorruptible, heaven-powered, and glory-driven.

Another of my favorite tombstones in the Middletown Springs cemetery is that of a fellow named Lamson Minor, who died September 2, 1806, at the age of thirty-two, certainly "before his time." His epitaph reads thusly:

> Sudden and unexpected I was summoned to this solitary
>     mansion.
> Ho, ho, beware, beware,
> For time is hastening.
> I shall soon awake on that consummate morn.

Lamson's just sleeping, brothers and sisters. He'll be waking soon, whenever it's get-up time.

# 10

# The Singular Miracle of the Eternally Begotten

"The works that I do in my Father's name bear witness about me" (John 10:25).

Jesus's miraculous control of nature reveals his glory as sovereign Master, his miraculous healings reveal his glory as Creator and restorer, his miraculous deliverances reveal his glory as Lord and Savior, and his miraculous raisings from the dead reveal his glory as the eternal God. All of the powerful signs of Christ point primarily to Christ. All of the miracles benefit others, but they are all self-referential.

So we miss the boat on the miracles when we get bogged down in discussions of attractional methodology, cessationism versus continuationism, and the like. All those are worthy subjects. But they miss the point of the mighty deeds, which is the proclamation of the mighty God and his kingdom.

Jesus performed many miracles, but he was essentially a miracle himself. We come now to the special case of Jesus himself, his very being and his miraculous self-revelations.

## The Incarnation

That the Bible proclaims the historical person Jesus of Nazareth to be the divine Son of God is, frankly, astonishing. Nevertheless,

Christians believe, as the Apostles' Creed affirms, "in Jesus Christ, [the Father's] only Son, our Lord." This divine title, "Lord," is given to Jesus as if he is God, *because he is God.*

How can this be? Why would we call a human being God? Did he become God? Was he born just like us and later transformed into or possessed by deity in some way?

The creed reminds us that Jesus "was conceived by the Holy Spirit, born of the virgin Mary." That short phrase summarizes the doctrine of the incarnation, which teaches this: Jesus was simultaneously both fully God and fully man. He was not God manifesting himself in the illusion or *appearance* of a man. And he was not man operating under the title "God" merely as a divine ambassador or adoptee. Jesus was—essentially, totally, and actually—God and man. The second person of the triune Godhead, the eternally begotten Son, took on human flesh.

The means of his incarnation is attributed in the Bible to the supernatural power of the Holy Spirit. Luke records the promise of Jesus's birth to his mother, Mary, this way:

> [T]he angel answered her, "The Holy Spirit will come upon you, and the power of the Most High will overshadow you; therefore the child to be born will be called holy—the Son of God." (Luke 1:35)

So Jesus had no earthly biological father, but of course he did have a biological mother, who was a virgin even when the Spirit caused the fertilization of the ovum within her, conceiving from the glory of heaven the divine zygote of the Son of God. This child grew to term like any other healthy child and was delivered to his parents. He had flesh and blood and all the normal bodily functions. He was weak and vulnerable; he needed to be fed and needed to grow and learn (Luke 2:52).

That Jesus was a real person who walked the earth is beyond all reasonable doubt. Ancient historians both religious and secular attest to his existence. But it is not Jesus's humanity that those who oppose the claims of Christian theology typically object to. It is not his birth to a young woman named Mary that so many reject. No, it is Jesus's divinity that sparks controversy. But the Scriptures are abundantly clear. Philippians 2:6 tells us Jesus had both the form of and equality with God. Colossians 1:15 tells us that Jesus is the image of God. First John 5:20 tells us that the Son is "the true God." In 2 Peter 1:1, the apostle refers to Jesus as "our God and Savior." In Acts 20:28, Paul says the church was purchased by the blood of God. Jesus himself proclaims, "I and the Father are one" (John 10:30), and lest we think he means simply that he and the Father are in agreement, we should point out that even the experts on the law recognized that this was a claim to deity (v. 33).

Of the claim that Jesus was born of a virgin, many critics today say this means simply that his mother was a young girl of marriageable age. This is true. But this is not the sense the biblical authors intend *virgin* to mean. Even if Isaiah could not have foreseen the full import of his prophecy (Isa. 7:14), Matthew gives us the fullness of meaning: "[Joseph] knew her not until she had given birth to a son" (1:25).

The biblical evidence for Jesus's deity is abundant. The fact that many Jews in the first century began to worship him as God ought to give us even more indication that the evidence of his divinity was felt to be quite strong, even overwhelming. But that has not stopped challenges throughout the centuries. No, in nearly every age, the orthodox church has had to respond to various forms of the ancient Arian heresy.

From the time of an Alexandrian priest named Arius in the late third and early fourth centuries, the incarnation of Jesus Christ has seemed a bridge too far. Arius denied the eternal deity of Jesus. His claim boiled down to the beliefs that Jesus was created by the Father and that the Son was of a *similar* essence to the Father, but not of the *same* essence. Arius denied that Jesus was the eternally begotten Son of God and instead said that there was a point in heavenly time when the Son was *unbegotten.*

The Council of Nicea was called largely to confront the Arian heresy, with the Alexandrian bishop Athanasius leading the charge. Athanasius provided the earliest, most powerful, and certainly most enduring defenses of the biblical truths of incarnational theology specifically and of Trinitarian doctrine in general. Grounded in the bold declarations of the epistles of the apostle John, Athanasius, in fact, categorized the Arian heresy as the work of the Antichrist.

We still deal with forms of Arius's damnable lies today. Nevertheless, orthodox Christianity always stands on Peter's hell-conquering confession that Jesus is "the Christ, the Son of the living God" (Matt. 16:16). We stand on what he said and what he *meant*.

We stand on this confession because we know that it is integral to Christ's gospel. To deny that Jesus was either fully God or fully man is to deny the salvation that Jesus the God-man has purchased. The incarnation is crucial to the good news of forgiveness of sins and the gift of eternal life. The reality is this: only man *should* pay the price for the sins of mankind, but only God *could* pay the price for the sins of mankind. Thus, in Jesus Christ, the "man should" and the "God could" unite in perfect payment and pure pardon.

The mathematics of the incarnation are inscrutable, of course. We aren't supposed to be able to wrap our finite minds around how the infinite God could also be a manifested, localized, killable man. It is surely a miracle. As such, it is meant to send us not into logic but into worship.

When Colossians 2:9 says, "For in him the whole fullness of deity dwells bodily," we are meant to stagger in wonder.

Will the Empire State Building occupy a doghouse? Will a killer whale fit inside an ant? Yet the Gospels tell us that omnipotence, omniscience, omnipresence, utter eternity, and holiness dwelled in a tiny, unformed person.

"The head of all rule and authority" (Col. 2:10) had one of those wobbly baby heads. The government rested on his baby-fatted shoulders (Isa. 9:6).

The miracle of the incarnation is vitally important to Christian faith. We must hold it tightly or we lose some of the majesty of

God's glory in Christ. God came as unborn child, as helpless babe, as dawdling toddler, as awkward teenager, as breathing, sweating, bleeding man so that Christ would experience all of humanity. And he experienced all of humanity so that we might receive all of him for all of us.

Surely if God came as a vulnerable, needful, weak baby, we have no need to fear for our own vulnerability, needfulness, and weakness. He emptied himself (Phil. 2:7) so that we would not see our own emptiness as a hopeless cause. "As you received Christ Jesus the Lord"—desperate, helpless, desirous—"so walk in him" (Col. 2:6). The miracle of the God-man proclaims the gospel's specialty: rescue of the helpless.

## The Transfiguration

It is a shame that we do not hear much teaching or preaching these days on the transfiguration of our Lord. To be sure, the texts that recount it are difficult and it is an intriguing and puzzling event in the ministry of Jesus, but there is something vitally important to be seen in this magnificent instance of self-revelation, something integral to the inauguration of the kingdom, the development of the church, and the life of Christian faith:

> And he said to them, "Truly, I say to you, there are some standing here who will not taste death until they see the kingdom of God after it has come with power."
>
> And after six days Jesus took with him Peter and James and John, and led them up a high mountain by themselves. And he was transfigured before them, and his clothes became radiant, intensely white, as no one on earth could bleach them. And there appeared to them Elijah with Moses, and they were talking with Jesus. And Peter said to Jesus, "Rabbi, it is good that we are here. Let us make three tents, one for you and one for Moses and one for Elijah." For he did not know what to say, for they were terrified. And a cloud overshadowed them, and a voice came out of the cloud, "This is my beloved Son;

listen to him." And suddenly, looking around, they no longer
saw anyone with them but Jesus only. (Mark 9:1–8)

It seems to me that what Jesus is referring to in verse 1 cannot be spun. I do not believe he is speaking metaphorically about
his second coming, but about his resurrection and ascension, and
the outpouring of the Spirit at the day of Pentecost. That is what
he means by seeing the kingdom of God coming with power, and
there are indeed many to whom he is speaking who will be present
for those events.

As a foretaste of this glory, however, perhaps as a way to bolster confidence and courage in the difficult days of the cross ahead,
Jesus takes his inner circle to a secluded, elevated place and gives
them a peek behind the curtain of his humanity. In what is called
his "transfiguration"––a transformation of his very person that
maintains continuity with his person—he opens the window wide
into heaven. For most of his life, Jesus's humanity has obscured
his divinity, but here in this moment, the reverse happens. Jesus's
humanity is eclipsed by a glimpse at his radiant glory.

The scene recollects a few major events in the Old Testament.
There is Moses after the command to leave Sinai, requesting to see
and seeing the glory of God (Ex. 33:18–23; 34:5–8). There is Isaiah's
encounter with the glory of God in the temple (Isa. 6:1–7). There
is also the fire from heaven sent down on Elijah's behalf (2 Kings 1)
and Elijah's being taken up into heaven (2 Kings 2). We could include other heavenly visions in the Old Testament, such as Jacob's
dream (Gen. 28:10–17) or many of Ezekiel's and Daniel's dreams.

All considered, we see that the patriarchs and the prophets
were given glimpses of heavenly glory that, like a patchwork quilt,
add up to completion in the divine revelation of Jesus Christ himself. He is the yes and amen of every dream, vision, and promise of
the ancient faithful (2 Cor. 1:20).

And lo and behold, "[T]here appeared to them Elijah with
Moses, and they were talking with Jesus" (Mark 9:4).

One of the interesting musings about the appearance of Elijah and Moses at Christ's transfiguration involves curiosity about their bodily presences in heaven. Elijah, as we know, didn't die but was taken up by God into heaven in a whirlwind (2 Kings 2:11). The death of Moses is more curious, as we are told that the Lord himself buried Moses and no one knew where his grave was (Deut. 34:1–6). That he died is not really in dispute—that seems clear enough from the text—but that his body was "handled" by God, that it was mysteriously hidden, and that it strangely is mentioned again in Jude 9, where we are told of Michael and Satan arguing over it, makes for very heady speculation.

What Elijah, Moses, and Jesus are talking about is not recorded. This lends credibility to the scene as an historical event (you might expect a fabricated scene to include some fabricated dialogue between the three). It is likely that the disciples cannot hear.

Peter, as he is wont to do, cannot *not* do something. He proposes a set of three tabernacles, one for each of their heavenly presences. He wants to make himself useful, and he is thinking theologically. A good Jew wants to be a good host to a manifestation of God's glory.

But Peter doesn't yet understand that Jesus is the tabernacle, that his incarnation is, in fact, the glory of God tabernacling with his people: "And the Word became flesh and dwelt [literally, *tabernacled*] among us, and we have seen his glory, glory as of the only Son from the Father, full of grace and truth" (John 1:14).

The last verse of the incident (Mark 9:8) is very important. Moses and Elijah, in effect, disappear. Only Jesus is left. As Moses and Elijah are representative of "the Law and the Prophets," writings that individually and collectively all point to Jesus, this moment in the transfiguration event is emblematic of Christ as the summation of all the Old Testament expectation. Jesus is the fulfillment of the Law and the Prophets. He is the embodiment of the transition from old covenant to new.

Jesus is himself the manifestation of God's law perfectly done, the lone worker of perfect righteousness. He is holiness personified. And Jesus is himself the manifestation of God's prophetic vision ecstatically, powerfully, and miraculously cast, the prophet who is the prophecy. Jesus is himself the Promised Land, the chariot of fire, the ultimate and only doorway into heaven. Jesus is the be-all and end-all.

He surpasses all of the Old Testament "heroes"; he subsumes them in his brilliance, as he is infinitely greater than they. He is the Passover lamb, the manna in the wilderness, the brazen serpent of Moses held aloft to heal all who will behold him.

He is the great high priest, surpassing all priests.

He is the good shepherd, surpassing all shepherds.

He is the great judge, surpassing all judges.

He is the King of kings, surpassing all kings.

He is the Lord of lords, surpassing all earthly masters.

He is the bridegroom, surpassing all husbands.

He is the Rabbi Christ, surpassing all preachers.

He is the alpha and omega, the beginning and the end, surpassing all the best of everyone, ever.

And thus it is now as it was then, that we should see only Jesus. Let us pray to the Father as the Greeks said to Philip, "Sir, we wish to see Jesus" (John 12:21).

What do we see when we see Jesus in his glory?

From the transfiguration event, we see, first, that Jesus doesn't just reflect glory—it emanates from him.

Second, we see that his righteousness, whiter than any man could manage, surpasses that of the Law and the Prophets, and certainly surpasses that of the Pharisees and scribes. Therefore, if we would have the righteousness to be taken to heaven, only owning Jesus's will do.

And third, we see that in eclipsing Moses and Elijah, Jesus proves himself not simply their replacement but their better.

Jesus is better. He is better than the law (Heb. 7:22). He "has obtained a ministry that is as much more excellent than the old as the covenant he mediates is better, since it is enacted on better promises" (Heb. 8:6). In Galatians 3:19–20, we learn that while the law's implementation required multiple intermediaries involved in a complex array of logistically difficult working parts, "God is one"—meaning, God saves us by himself. God saves us from himself, through himself, to himself, by himself, for himself. "The gospel," writes William Cooper, "so much exceeds in glory, that it eclipses the glory of the legal, as the stars disappear when the sun ariseth, and goeth forth in his strength."[1]

That the law could be fulfilled, what a miracle!

The law is good, but Jesus is better. The law is good because it is from God, and it is good for what God meant it to do. It is good in the way a correct diagnosis is good. But while the law is good like a diagnosis is good, Jesus is better than the law like a cure is better than a diagnosis.

The miracle of the transfiguration, then, while historical, is also symbolic of the miracle of God's forgiveness of sins, removal of the burden of the law, and imputation of Christ's righteousness to sinners.

## The Resurrection

The miracles are heating up now. And the hottest revelation of all comes when blood runs most cold.

The disciples are in mourning. For three long days, they are shocked, confused, distraught. Even after all Jesus has taught them, plainly telling them at several points that he must die and be raised, they have heard him but have not really heard him. Turns out, he was right about the death. But the notion of a resurrection does not seem to be even a glimmer in the musings of Jesus's grieving friends.

But then comes a rumor. Then a stirring. Then a report from the tomb. Then Jesus himself is standing before them.

The amazement eclipses the reaction to all Jesus's miracles put together, for his resurrection eclipses all of his miracles put together.

---

[1] From William Cooper's preface to Jonathan Edwards, *Distinguishing Marks of a Work of the Spirit of God,* in *The Works of President Edwards,* vol. 1 (New York: Leavitt and Allen, 1852), 519.

The apostle Paul preaches the resurrection of Jesus plainly and exultantly: "But in fact Christ has been raised from the dead" (1 Cor. 15:20).

There is no beating around the bush of that phrase "in fact." The resurrection the apostles proclaimed, the one that we, the Christian church, proclaim, was not a symbolic, metaphorical, ahistorical event. As the miracles actually happened—matter changing, objects appearing from nonexistence—Jesus's return from the grave was no illusion. This was not a spiritualization. He did not resurrect "in the hearts" of his followers.

One of my favorite Easter reflections is this poetic doozy from novelist John Updike. His "Seven Stanzas at Easter" is wondrous and makes a crucial point, powerfully:

> Make no mistake: if He rose at all
> it was as His body;
> if the cells' dissolution did not reverse, the molecules
> reknit, the amino acids rekindle,
> the Church will fall.

Updike goes on to say:

> Let us not mock God with metaphor,
> analogy, sidestepping transcendence;
> making of the event a parable, a sign painted in the
> faded credulity of earlier ages:
> let us walk through the door.

> The stone is rolled back, not papier-mâché,
> not a stone in a story,
> but the vast rock of materiality that in the slow
> grinding of time will eclipse for each of us
> the wide light of day.

> And if we will have an angel at the tomb,
> make it a real angel,

weighty with Max Planck's quanta, vivid with hair,
opaque in the dawn light, robed in real linen
spun on a definite loom.

Let us not seek to make it less monstrous,
for our own convenience, our own sense of beauty,
lest, awakened in one unthinkable hour, we are
embarrassed by the miracle,
and crushed by remonstrance.[2]

The mockery of metaphor is unfortunately employed in many churches on Easter Sunday, and it certainly appears on the covers of well-timed newsmagazines aiming to throw the cold water of skepticism on the "deluded" masses. But as Updike says, if the resurrection is not real, the church will fall.

My death will not be symbolic. It will be real. Therefore, a metaphorical resurrection is no hope for me. I am looking forward to those rekindled amino acids.

This is exactly what Christ's resurrection miracle means for us: a resurrection of our own! As in the miracle of the fish and the loaves, Jesus presents his own body as the miraculous offering for a glorious multiplication of resurrections in the last day. In this vein, Paul, continuing in 1 Corinthians 15:20, calls the risen Christ "the firstfruits of those who have fallen asleep."

This is just the beginning!

But each in his own order: Christ the firstfruits, then at his coming those who belong to Christ. (v. 23)

Jesus purchases eternal life for us at the cross and proves its results in his resurrection, which shows us what awaits those who are in Christ. Paul is giving us here an end-times order, and on his short fold-out illustrative chart, Christ's resurrection is the beginning of the end!

[2] John Updike, "Seven Stanzas at Easter," in *Telephone Poles and Other Poems* (New York: Alfred A. Knopf, 1963), 72–73.

Jesus, now ascended, will return in the future.
Then the dead in Christ will be raised.

Then comes the end, when he delivers the kingdom to God the Father after destroying every rule and every authority and power. (v. 24)

He changes our status, liberating us finally from the usurping rule of our flesh. He changes our vision, liberating us from the temptation of the idols we worship. He changes our belonging, liberating us from the power of sin and death itself, declaring with his consummated lordship over our hearts, souls, and minds, "Mine!"

He saves the worst for last:

For he must reign until he has put all his enemies under his feet. The last enemy to be destroyed is death. (vv. 25–26)

The resurrection proves that not even death escapes Christ's lordship. He kills sin at the cross, disarming all the spiritual rulers and authorities. And in conquering the grave, he emerges with the keys to death in his triumphant fist.

By going into death and coming back out, transformed and victorious, Christ changes our destiny, so that death, decay, and decomposition are not just trifles but effectively nonissues.

Ever since the fall, everything has been winding down, dying and decaying. But since the advent of the gospel of Christ's life, death, and resurrection, Jesus has been building his kingdom so that the Father's will will be done on earth as it is in heaven. Creation will be restored to "better than good," to an endless stage more glorious than it was before Adam sinned.

We will not be disembodied spirits prancing about the ether of some outer-spatial heaven. We will need new bodies with which to dance, sing, worship, work, play, love, laugh, eat, drink, run, swim, and on and on, forever and ever.

So Jesus will give these new bodies to us:

Behold! I tell you a mystery. We shall not all sleep, but we shall all be changed, in a moment, in the twinkling of an eye, at the last trumpet. For the trumpet will sound, and the dead will be raised imperishable, and we shall be changed. (vv. 51–52)

We are not going into death (except in our dying bodies). We are more accurately heading toward life! Things are looking up!

Our resurrection bodies will be like Christ's resurrection body, which could apparently both eat breakfast (John 21:15) and walk through walls (20:19, 26). It looked like him (vv. 19–20) but didn't look like him (Luke 24:15–16). Our resurrection bodies will be us, but the *real* us, the true us, the us we were meant to be, the us revealed in Christ and reflective of him. We will finally be really alive. As Dwight Moody once quipped: "Someday you will read in the papers that D. L. Moody of East Northfield is dead. Don't you believe a word of it! At that moment I shall be more alive than I am now."[3]

For this perishable body must put on the imperishable, and this mortal body must put on immortality. When the perishable puts on the imperishable, and the mortal puts on immortality, then shall come to pass the saying that is written:

"Death is swallowed up in victory."
"O death, where is your victory?
O death, where is your sting?"

The sting of death is sin, and the power of sin is the law. But thanks be to God, who gives us the victory through our Lord Jesus Christ. (1 Cor. 15:53–57)

As we have seen in Jesus's words in his resurrection miracles, the Christian's vision of death requires a radical overhaul, a redefinition. We think of death now as a kind of sleep, having moved from fearing death to actually mocking it.

[3] D. L. Moody, cited in Timothy George, "Introduction: Remembering Mr. Moody," in *Mr. Moody and the Evangelical Tradition*, ed. Timothy George (New York: Continuum, 2005), 1.

Therefore, if I am overcome by suffering, in deep pain, on the verge of dying, and unsure of when my number may be called, I should despair *if Christ is not risen*. From his deathbed, Jaroslav Pelikan is said to have declared: "If Christ is risen, nothing else matters. And if Christ is not—nothing else matters."[4]

But if Christ is risen, I know that I will gain him in an overwhelmingly satisfying way at my death. I will be climactically "found in him." Christ's resurrection means that my death, in faith, will precipitate an enduring, infinite miracle of my own.

## The Ascension

Like Christ's transfiguration, his ascension is another miraculous event not given nearly enough coverage in the evangelical world. But the event is integral to our faith and to the continuing existence of Christianity:

> So when they had come together, they asked him, "Lord, will you at this time restore the kingdom to Israel?" He said to them, "It is not for you to know times or seasons that the Father has fixed by his own authority. But you will receive power when the Holy Spirit has come upon you, and you will be my witnesses in Jerusalem and in all Judea and Samaria, and to the end of the earth." And when he had said these things, as they were looking on, he was lifted up, and a cloud took him out of their sight. And while they were gazing into heaven as he went, behold, two men stood by them in white robes, and said, "Men of Galilee, why do you stand looking into heaven? This Jesus, who was taken up from you into heaven, will come in the same way as you saw him go into heaven." (Acts 1:6–11)

The ascension of Christ, in fact, is a rich well of miraculous power from which we may draw incredibly encouraging sustenance.

---

[4] "In Memoriam: Faculty," Yale Department of History Newsletter (Spring 2007), 3. (Available online: http://www.learningace.com/doc/2851196/4f2988fe924110ed3ce00f5f1315b7bd/historynewsletter07f).

For instance, first we see from this event that Jesus is really alive. We see that he is still alive, that he is reigning even now and will live forever. The reality of Christ's ascension, inextricable from the resurrection event, tells us that he did not rise from the dead only to die again later like Lazarus, Jairus's daughter, the widow of Nain's son, Tabitha, and Eutychus. Jesus's body will not be found because he took its glorified tangibility to heaven.

Second, the ascension tells us something mind-blowing about the nature of heaven itself—namely, that heaven is a "thicker" reality than earth. We tend to think of heaven as the ethereal place of disembodied spirits. And in a way, it is. But Elijah is there. And Enoch. And so is the risen, glorified, *incarnate* Christ. Jesus is there, taking up material space. He is touchable, present. Clearly, heaven is not less real than earth but more. The ascension of Christ's resurrected body to the hyper-spatial presence of God's glory reveals that heaven is a thicker reality than our four-dimensional space, more vibrant, more colorful, more real. It is the spiritual plane, but physical matter nevertheless may take up space there!

Third, the ascension of Christ's glorified, incarnate body reveals that God's plan for human dominion is being realized. This is what I mean:

The first Adam and his helper, Eve, were charged with filling the earth and subduing it. Obviously, they screwed up this mandate. But God's plans will not be thwarted. Man *will* reflect God's glory in dominion over creation, because it is God's will for him to do so. In the incarnation, then, God sends his only Son to right the course, reverse the curse, and begin the restoration of all things. The second Adam (Christ) does the job, and even in his glorification, the incarnational miracle persists, fulfilling God's plan for man to reflect divine glory in dominion over creation. The God-man, who is the radiance of the glory of God, rules over the earth and is even now subduing his enemies. As Tim Keller says, "[T]he ascension means there is a human being ruling the universe."[5]

---

[5] Timothy Keller, "The Ascension," sermon on Acts 1:1–12, May 18, 1997. Audio available at http://thegospel coalition.org/resources/entry/The-Ascension.

Fourth, the ascension of Jesus means that the incarnation is an *enduring* miracle.

The incarnation was a humbling of God's Son, but not a lessening of him. The Son of God even maintained his omnipresence throughout his incarnation![6] (Historical theologians have traditionally called this perspective the *extra calvinisticum*.) But the ascension means that Jesus Christ forever remains the Christ who is Jesus. He did not revert back to intangibility. His ascended incarnational state, then, is not an eternal limitation but a part of his ongoing efforts to fill all things (Eph. 4:10). He takes up *more* space in the heavens and the earth now, not less. This means that the incarnation is a miracle with no expiration date.

Finally, the point of the ascension is the point of Jesus himself: glory for God in the good news for sinners. The ascension is gospel!

Why? Because if, among the many things the gospel means, it means we are united with Christ through faith, it also means that where he is we will be also. It means we will go to heaven in spirit and heaven will come to us in body. The ascension is the full fruition of the promise of Christ's resurrection being the forerunner of our own. The ascension means the gospel is better news than we even thought, gooder than good! It holds out the promise, the blessed hope, not just of life after death, but, as N. T. Wright says, "life *after* 'life after death.'"[7]

What a gracious God we have!

---

[6] I have expounded on this concept more fully in *Gospel Deeps: Reveling in the Excellencies of Jesus* (Wheaton, IL: Crossway, 2012), 139–48.

[7] N. T. Wright, *The Resurrection of the Son of God* (Minneapolis, MN: Fortress, 2003), 86.

# Conclusion

Therefore, Christians, let us never forget that Christianity is supernatural. God is dealing with and saving the natural man, having come and become a natural man (though without sin and without relinquishing his deity), but what started us, sustains us, and will save us is not what we might call "natural."

Our boredom at any time, then, is a sin. Sin is, at its essence, a failure of worship, and failing to worship is failing to be astonished by the presence and activity of God in the world. Sin is a failure to marvel at and be motivated by the miracle of the gospel.

The Roman Catholic Church's original criticism of the Reformation movement included its alleged lack of miraculous signs. John Calvin replied to these charges by saying, first of all, that the Reformation was not new but merely a continuation of the apostolic preaching of the gospel, and, further, that this gospel—the news that God saves sinners through the life, death, and resurrection of Jesus Christ—is miracle enough.

And it is. This is even the point of all of Jesus's varied signs and wonders. "I am enough," he is saying. "I am enough for security, I am enough for provision, I am enough for restoration, I am enough for freedom, I am enough for life." As we see in so many of his miracles, in fact, he is *more* than enough.

In the miracles, we see Jesus as he was, is, and evermore shall be. His glory is revealed in them, so many gleaming facets of the diamond of his finished work, so many roaring waves of the oceans of his mighty power, so many resounding notes of the music of his saving message.

Miracle by miracle, in the Gospels, we see that the people who got it *got it*. They were overcome with how supernatural life had just become because they had placed their faith in Jesus. Their hearts were alight, their souls ringing with the echoes of eternity. They fell down, they danced, they marveled, they trembled.

It is this reaction to the ongoing miracle of the gospel that Paul commands in Philippians 2:12–13:

> Therefore, my beloved, as you have always obeyed, so now, not only as in my presence but much more in my absence, work out your own salvation with fear and trembling, for it is God who works in you, both to will and to work for his good pleasure.

"Fear and trembling." Paul uses this phrase elsewhere twice (2 Cor. 7:15; Eph. 6:5), apparently with the connotation of submissive humility and receptive meekness. The phrase refers to being "put in one's place," yet in a way that activates all of our affections toward God, not simply "fear." "Fear and trembling" captures the disposition appropriate to the circumstances. The command in Psalm 2:11 is to "serve the Lord with fear, and rejoice with trembling," showing us that fear is not without activity and trembling is not without joy.

Here I remember Emma Thompson's beautiful portrayal of Elinor Dashwood at the end of the Ang Lee film adaptation of Jane Austen's *Sense and Sensibility*, when Hugh Grant's Edward Ferrars reveals it was his brother who got married, not himself. Thompson's Elinor is an expert at keeping her emotions bottled up—until this moment, when we see "fear and trembling" brilliantly and movingly on display. It chokes me up every time. It is a picture to me of my gospel wakefulness, the overwhelming, climactic, life-changing moment when, while I was hiding in the rubble of my life, God's glory passed by. The atmosphere of the gospel of grace freshly entered *me*.

What may happen when the miracle of the gospel lands squarely in your heart, when it becomes real, the reality that God—as in, *God*—loves you?

Pent-up hopes and dormant affections are brought near the super-electric current of a fearsome reality. The hair on our arms stands up, gooseflesh springing, a sense of fresh air and being winded at the same time. Overwhelmed: that's fear and trembling. As it pertains to having the living God draw near to us, the experience of fear and trembling assumes it is truly God and the glorious Christ we have encountered and not some pitiful caricature. The god of the prosperity gospelists is a pathetic doormat, a genie. The god of the cutesy coffee mugs and Joel Osteen tweets is a milquetoast doofus like the guys in the Austen novels you hope the girls *don't* end up with, holding their hats limply in hand and minding their manners to follow your lead like a butler—or the doormat he stands on. The god of the American Dream is Santa Claus. The god of the open theists is not sovereignly omniscient, declaring the end from the beginning, but just a really good guesser playing the odds. The god of our therapeutic culture is ourselves, we, the "forgivers" of ourselves, navel-haloed morons with "baggage" but not sin. None of these pathetic gods could provoke fear and trembling.

But the God of the Scriptures is a consuming fire (Deut. 4:24). "It is a fearful thing to fall into the hands of the living God" (Heb. 10:31). He stirs up the oceans with the tip of his finger, and they sizzle rolling clouds of steam into the sky. He shoots lightning from his fists. This is the God who leads his children by a pillar of cloud and a pillar of fire. This is the God who makes war, sends plagues, and sits enthroned in majesty and glory in his heavens, doing what he pleases. This is the God who, in the flesh, turned tables over in the temple as if he owned the place. This Lord God Jesus Christ was pushed to the edge of the cliff and declared, "This is not happening today," and walked right back through the crowd like a boss. This Lord says, "No one takes my life; I give it willingly," as if to say, "You couldn't kill me unless I let you." This Lord calms the storms, casts out demons, binds and looses, and has the authority to grant us the ability to do the same. The Devil is this God's lapdog.

And it is *this* God who has summoned us, apprehended us, saved us. It is this God who has come humbly, meekly, lowly, pouring out his blood in infinite conquest to set the captives free, cancel the record of debt against us, conquer sin and Satan, and swallow up death forever.

Let us, then, advance the gospel of the kingdom out into the perimeter of our hearts and lives with affectionate meekness and humble submission. Let us repent of our nonchalance. Let us embrace the wonder of Christ.

# General Index

# Scripture Index